Thank God!! :)
We're debt free!!
$83,900 in
20 months
—Jesse + Jenn

Michelle Sinkovitz,
35K in 15 months!
Thank you so much
Dave! You are really
an inspiration to
so many!

[?] [?] [?]
days! We're
debt free!!
Erin & Kevin
Phoenix, AZ

Kyle + Amber White
$36,000 in 7 months!
Say NO to debt!!

$ 51,000 PAID OFF
AT 51 YEARS OLD!
I am debt free!
Elaine Davide

WE'RE DEBT FREE!
THANKS FOR EVERYTHING
DAVE!
Mike & Cathy

To God Be The Glory!
We're Debt FREE!!!
The Schmersal Family!
$120,000.00 Paid off 34 mths.
Wiiiia   Luke   Rob ♡ Anji
         Faith Lydia
      Rebekah

Debt free!
—Jen & Jim

Dave and Kim Monk (Troy, IL)
$137,000 in 3½ years!
* including our home! ☺
☑ Baby step 6

We're debt free!
119,500/35 mo
We did it, So can you
Stephanie & David [?]

THIS BOOK BELONGS TO

Enshané Nomoto

START DATE
THE DAY YOU DECIDED TO CHANGE (again)

4 / 6 / 2019

MONTH | DAY | YEAR

We've all done stupid. I did stupid with zeros on the end.

I started from nothing. But by the time I was 26 I had a net worth of a little over a million dollars. And then it all came crashing down.

The short story? I had a lot of debt. And it caused me to lose everything. That was the bottom for me.

You might be on your way to the bottom. You might already be there. Or maybe you were the smart one who didn't borrow money at all. No matter where you are, you can always do better.

And you're not alone.

I discovered God's and Grandma's ways of handling money and learned that the only way to change my situation was to change the guy in my mirror. So, I changed. It was a long, painful process, but it worked. And it will work for you too.

For more than two decades, over five million people have found success with the same proven plan that you're about to follow. Stick with us, stay focused, and follow each step, and I promise, you *will* change your life.

If you'll live like no one else now, later you can live and give like no one else.

You got this! It's game on.

THE 7 BABY STEPS

OUR *Proven* PLAN

If you want to win with money, you can't do what you've always done. You need a plan that works. That's why Dave created the 7 Baby Steps. It's a clear path to know where you are and where you're headed next. This isn't a get-rich-quick scheme, and you haven't won the lottery. But if you follow each step—in order and with great focus and intentionality—you will change your life.

BABY STEP 1
Save $1,000 for Your Starter Emergency Fund

BABY STEP 2
Pay Off All Debt (Except the House) Using the Debt Snowball

BABY STEP 3
Save 3–6 Months of Expenses in a Fully Funded Emergency Fund

BABY STEP 4
Invest 15% of Your Household Income in Retirement

BABY STEP 5
Save for Your Children's College Fund

BABY STEP 6
Pay Off Your Home Early

BABY STEP 7
Build Wealth and Give

COURSE OVERVIEW

You've learned the Baby Steps, but that's not the whole course!
You've got nine video lessons ahead of you. The first four
will walk you through our proven plan, the 7 Baby Steps.
And the last five lessons will teach you how to
tackle life on the plan. Let's break it down.

BABY STEPS 4 5 6 7
Page 58

LESSON 04

BABY STEP 3
Page 44

LESSON 03

BABY STEP 2
Page 28

LESSON 02

BABY STEP 1 & BUDGETING
Page 12

LESSON 01

The PLAN

Lessons 1–4 walk you through the 7
Baby Steps. This is your proven plan to
win with money. In these lessons, you'll
learn how to do more than just treat
the symptoms of your money problem.
You'll get to the root of the problem:
your behavior!

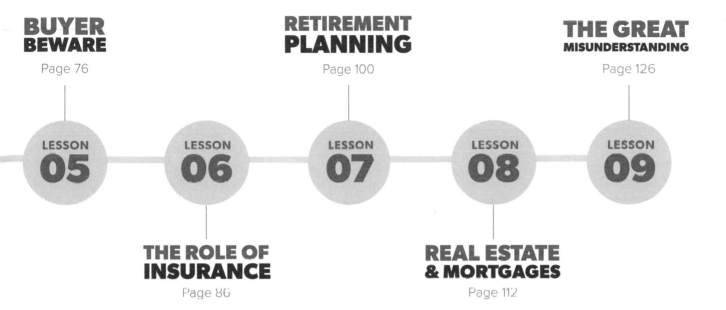

BUYER BEWARE

RETIREMENT PLANNING

THE GREAT MISUNDERSTANDING

LESSON **05**

LESSON **06**

LESSON **07**

LESSON **08**

LESSON **09**

THE ROLE OF INSURANCE

REAL ESTATE & MORTGAGES

Life ON THE PLAN

Lessons 5–9 keep you on track with the Baby Steps. Learn to navigate spending, insurance, real estate, and investing, so you don't ruin your progress! And protect yourself from everything trying to get at your money, so you can start fighting for the things you want.

MEET *the* TEAM

Whether you've done stupid with zeros on the end or you're just trying to do a little better, we know that money is a big deal in your life. You may feel ashamed. You may just feel stressed. And if you're not scared, you're probably a little unsure of what to do with your money and where it can take you.

That's why we have a team who's been where you are right now, knows how to win with money, and will help you get there too.

Dave Ramsey, Chris Hogan, and Rachel Cruze are all #1 best-selling authors who speak to sold-out venues across the country. Their books, podcasts, and shows have helped millions of people change their lives. And today, they're going to help you change yours.

DAVE RAMSEY

After battling his way out of bankruptcy and millions of dollars in debt, he started on a mission to make sure other people discovered the way out. That's why he created *Financial Peace University*. Today, over five million people have experienced life-change through this course. And he's helped millions more through his seven best-selling books, countless live events hosted across the nation, and his radio show, *The Dave Ramsey Show*, heard by more than fourteen million listeners each week. Dave's biblical, commonsense advice is for anyone ready to win with money.

"Live like no one else SO LATER YOU CAN LIVE AND GIVE LIKE NO ONE ELSE."

Chris HOGAN

While helping clients at a well-respected mortgage company, Chris Hogan felt powerless as he watched people throw away their financial futures. That's when he met Dave Ramsey. For the last decade, Chris has been on our team, on a mission to help millions like you make their money dreams a reality.

Chris is an expert on retirement and wealth building. He's a #1 national best-selling author, dynamic speaker, and financial coach—which means he's seen it all! His newest book is *Everyday Millionaires: How Ordinary People Built Extraordinary Wealth—And How You Can Too.*

"ANYONE IN THIS COUNTRY CAN *become a millionaire.* I CAN SHOW YOU HOW."

Rachel CRUZE

Rachel Cruze grew up learning how to win with money. As Dave Ramsey's daughter, she was taught from an early age how to give generously, spend wisely, and save for the future. She understands the dangers of debt, and she's seen firsthand the damage it can do. But as she'll tell you, she's also a spender and hated budgeting until she learned what a budget can really do!

Rachel has authored three best-selling books, is a #1 *New York Times* best-selling author, and is host of *The Rachel Cruze Show*. But what is she most known for? Fun! Rachel is an energetic, personable speaker who wants you to handle your money with wisdom, so you can live a life you love.

"A BUDGET DOESN'T LIMIT YOUR FREEDOM. *A budget gives you freedom."*

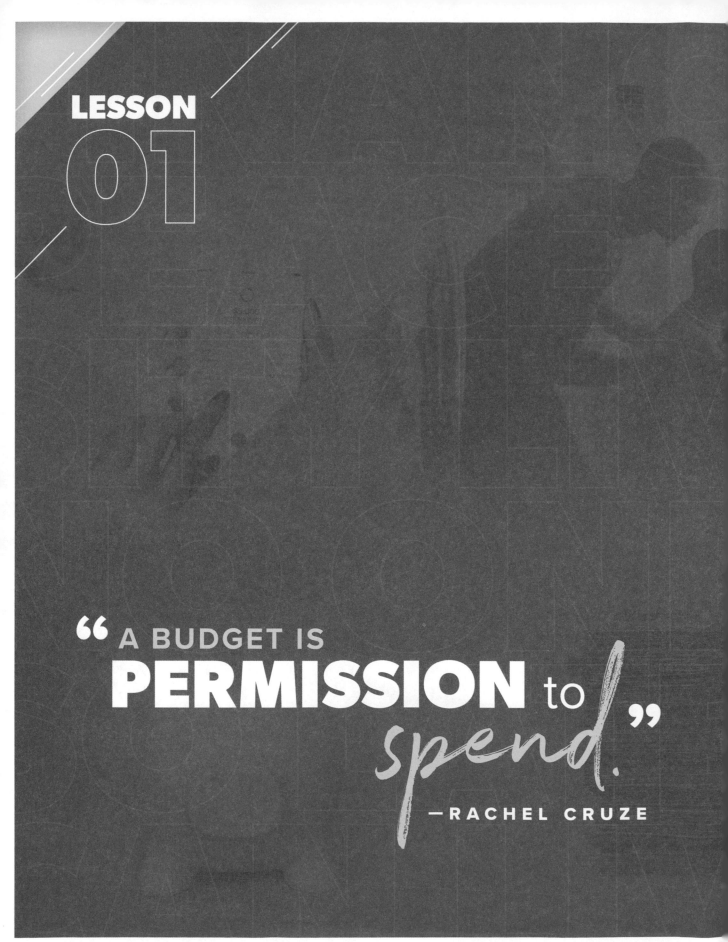

LESSON
01

" A BUDGET IS **PERMISSION** to *spend.* "

—RACHEL CRUZE

BABY STEP 1
&BUDGETING

KEY POINTS

The 7 Baby Steps focus on changing your behavior toward money through a proven, step-by-step plan.

Baby Step 1 is saving $1,000 for your starter emergency fund.

A zero-based budget is the tool that helps you take control of your money.

BABY STEP

1

Save $1,000 for Your Starter Emergency Fund

Your first goal is to save $1,000 for your starter emergency fund as fast as you possibly can. Saving has to become a priority. Focus all of your energy on getting this Baby Step done—fast! An emergency is going to happen, so you have to be ready when it hits. We're talking no credit cards, but real cash in the bank to cover it.

LESSON 1 //
BABY STEP 1

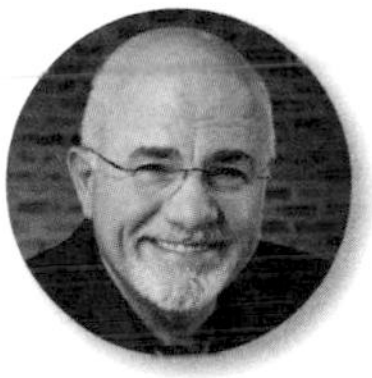

GUIDE
Dave Ramsey

BABY STEP 1

Save ________ for your starter emergency fund.

If you will live like no one else now, later you can live and ________ like no one else.

> **NO DISCIPLINE SEEMS PLEASANT AT THE TIME, BUT PAINFUL. LATER ON, HOWEVER, IT PRODUCES A** *harvest of righteousness and peace* **FOR THOSE WHO HAVE BEEN TRAINED BY IT.**
>
> HEBREWS 12:11 (NIV)

Notes

ANSWER KEY

$1,000
Give

GUIDE
Rachel Cruze

BUDGETING

Give it _____ _____ to get into a rhythm.

The _____ enjoys doing the budget.

The _____ _____ feels controlled by the budget.

In the Budget Committee _____, you will meet with your spouse to review the next month's budget.

The budget gives you _____ you never knew you had.

> **SUPPOSE ONE OF YOU WANTS TO BUILD A TOWER.**
> # WON'T YOU FIRST SIT DOWN AND ESTIMATE THE COST
> **TO SEE IF YOU HAVE ENOUGH MONEY TO** *complete it?*
>
> — LUKE 14:28 (NIV)

Notes

It must be a zero-based budget. That means your income minus expenses equals _____,

The _____ _____ are food, utilities, shelter, and transportation.

Take control of your money by creating your EveryDollar budget at **financialpeace.com**.

one-minute
TAKEAWAY

_____

_____

_____

_____

_____

_____

NERD & Free Spirit QUIZ

WHAT TO DO:

Take this fun quiz to figure out if you're more of a Nerd or a Free Spirit! If you're married, this will help you identify your role in the Budget Committee Meeting. If you're single, this will help you determine your strengths in creating your budget, and where you'll need some accountability.

PERSON 1
A   B

PICK THE ONE THAT SOUNDS MOST LIKE YOU!

PERSON 2
A   B

A: You're prepared for Tax Day months in advance.
B: Tax Day? That's in October, right?

A: Rules are important and should always be followed.
B: Rules are more like suggestions.

A: You are always on time. Always.
B: You show up "on time," give or take 15 minutes.

A: You make a plan for each day of your vacation.
B: Vacations are more fun with no schedule.

A: You read the introductions of books.
They're in there for a reason!
B: You skip introductions—only chapters count.

A: Your life's motto: "A place for everything
and everything in its place."
B: You live by the phrase, "It'll all work out!"

A: You organize your shirts by color. Doesn't everyone?
B: You're doing good just to get your shirts off the floor.

A: You can't wait to create your EveryDollar budget!
*B: You're considering faking an illness for the
Budget Committee Meeting.*

A   B
← **TOTAL YOUR SCORES AND CIRCLE THE HIGHEST ONE** →
A   B

IF YOU HAD A HIGH SCORE OF: A

SCORE

4–5: NERD-ISH
You have a pretty good idea of how much money is in your account.

6–7: NERD
Budgets are for awesome people.

8: ULTRA NERD
You canceled your plans with friends so you could start drafting next month's budget.

IF YOU HAD A HIGH SCORE OF: B

SCORE

4–5: FREE SPIRIT-ISH
You've got a budget somewhere. You could find it if you needed to.

6–7: FREE SPIRIT
Budgets are for boring people.

8: ULTRA FREE SPIRIT
Budgets are like putting on a straitjacket. Why would you ever do that to yourself?

OFFICIAL RULES OF THE
BUDGET COMMITTEE
MEETING

FOR THE NERD

1. Create the budget.
2. Thank the Free Spirit for being there!
3. Show the budget to the Free Spirit. Then be quiet.

FOR THE FREE SPIRIT

1. Come to the Budget Committee Meeting.
2. Be realistic and don't use the phrase "whatever you think."
3. Have an opinion and change something.

WHAT TO DO:

Fill out your estimated monthly expenses for the following categories. Then add up the total for all categories.

SEE WHAT YOU'RE *Spending*

Now that you know whether you're more of a Nerd or a Free Spirit, it's time to take the first step into budgeting. Don't panic, this first step is simple!

THE BUDGET IS YOUR MAP FOR THE MONTH

Rachel taught you how to create a zero-based budget with EveryDollar. But to get to where you want to go, you have to know where you are.

It's just like driving: If you don't know your starting point, it's impossible to get to your destination! That's why you do a **Quick-Start Budget.**

IT'S TIME TO FILL OUT THE QUICK-START BUDGET

This activity is a simple way to put pen to paper and get you thinking about how much you're currently spending in each category, each month. You'll notice there are a few categories missing, like income and debt. That's okay! Remember, this is just your starting point.

Free Spirits,
make sure there is
fun in the budget!

Nerds,
this is where you get to work with numbers!

☐ STEP 1

Write down what you're spending for the month in each item of each category. If you don't know exact numbers, just make your best guess!

☐ STEP 2

Add up each item in each category and write the TOTAL at the bottom.

☐ STEP 3

Add up the numbers in all of the TOTAL boxes and write that number in the TOTAL FOR CATEGORIES box.

YOUR QUICK-START BUDGET

Follow Steps 1–3 on the previous page to list and add up your monthly expenses.

♥ GIVING — Planned

	Planned
Church	
Charity	
TOTAL	

🍴 FOOD — Planned

	Planned
Groceries	
Restaurants	
TOTAL	

👕 PERSONAL — Planned

	Planned
Clothing	
Phone	
Fun Money	
Gifts	
TOTAL	

🚚 TRANSPORTATION — Planned

	Planned
Auto Insurance	
Gas & Oil	
Maintenance	
TOTAL	

🏠 HOUSING — Planned

	Planned
Mortgage/Rent	
Utilities	
TOTAL	

TOTAL FOR CATEGORIES	

Remember, this total does not include every category that will be in your monthly budget—just a few of the big ones!

Great Start!

You've taken the first step to creating your monthly budget. In the Action Steps, you'll **create a zero-based budget with EveryDollar—just like Rachel showed you!**

DISCUSSION

This is where change happens—in a safe space where you can talk about real life. This is where you *start* connecting with other people and *stop* believing you're in this alone. Whether you're in a group or online, be honest with your answers and remember to encourage the people around you!

 Think about a time when an emergency stressed you out. How would a starter emergency fund have made that a *stress-free* emergency?

 What are some categories that you think might bust your budget? What can you do to keep those categories under control?

 Cashing out your budget can help you stay ahead of problem categories. Which categories could you use envelopes or clips for to help you stick to your budget?

 Based on your results from the Nerd & Free Spirit Quiz, what strengths can you bring to the Budget Committee Meeting?

KEEP THE CONVERSATION GOING!

Answer these questions online in the Financial Peace community!

financialpeace.com

ACTION STEPS

Personal finance is 80% behavior. It's only 20% head knowledge.
So it's time to live out what you just learned! Complete each of the
action steps before the next lesson. (If you're married, do this with
your spouse.) You got this!

☐ **KNOCK OUT BABY STEP 1**
It's time to draw a line in the sand. This is when you decide
to change. Baby Step 1 is saving $1,000 for your starter
emergency fund. Use the Emergency Fund Planner on
financialpeace.com to get that cash in the bank as fast as you
can! If you've already got your $1,000, well done! Move on to
the next Action Step.

☐ **CREATE A BUDGET WITH EVERYDOLLAR**
Your Quick-Start Budget was a great way to get the hang of
budgeting. Now, create a zero-based budget with **EveryDollar.**
Married couples, don't forget the Budget Committee Meeting.
And singles, show your budget to your accountability partner
and ask for feedback. If you have an irregular income or
want to budget weekly, use the Irregular Income or Allocated
Spending forms on **financialpeace.com**. Examples of these
forms are on pages 140–145.

☐ **COMPLETE YOUR FINANCIAL SNAPSHOT**
Use the Financial Snapshot tool at **financialpeace.com** to list
your debt, savings, and active credit cards. If you're in a group,
transfer that information to the Financial Snapshot card (page
24) and turn it in to your coordinator at the start of Lesson 2.

☐ **READ *THE POWERFUL ZERO-BASED BUDGET* ON THE
NEXT PAGE**
The only way to control your money is with a budget—a
zero-based budget. Want a quick refresher on how to easily
make one with EveryDollar? Read on!

THE *Powerful* ZERO-BASED BUDGET

Whether you're on Baby Step 1 or 7, you need a budget. It's your map for every month. And it puts you in control of your money.

Want to pay off debt? *You need a budget.* Want to build your emergency fund? *You need a budget.* Already investing? You're not off the hook—*you still need a budget.* And not just any budget—that's right, a zero-based budget.

A zero-based budget simply means your income minus your expenses equals zero. One more time: Your income minus *everything else* equals zero. That means you give every dollar a job to do—every month. *Hint: That's why we named our tool EveryDollar.* Plan on purpose for every dollar, every month!

1 **START WITH YOUR INCOME**

2 **LIST ALL YOUR EXPENSES**

3 **SUBTRACT EXPENSES FROM INCOME**

4 **TRACK YOUR EXPENSES**

5 **BE FLEXIBLE!**

HOW TO DO A MONTHLY BUDGET

1 **START WITH YOUR INCOME**
Write down all the income you expect
for the month.

INCOME	
Paycheck	$3,500

2 **LIST ALL YOUR EXPENSES**
Remember what Rachel said: This is
everything under income, from giving to
miscellaneous!

 EXPENSES	
Giving	$350
Saving	$450
Rent	$875
Utilities	$350
Groceries/Restaurants	$525
Transportation	$350
Insurance	$500
Miscellaneous	$100

3 **SUBTRACT EXPENSES FROM INCOME**
If your income minus your expenses
equals zero, you did it! You've just made a
zero-based budget. If it doesn't, you've got
some work to do! Adjust some categories
and get to zero.

	INCOME
−	EXPENSES
=	**$0**

4 **TRACK YOUR EXPENSES**
Track your expenses every day during
the month to make sure you're sticking to
your budget. If you're overspending, make
adjustments in your categories and then
learn to say no!

5 **BE FLEXIBLE!**
Planning for payments shows you just how much debt steals your income! Let's say you
have a car payment of $325 and a student loan payment of $150. You need to include
those debts in your budget and adjust other categories to account for those expenses.
Remember, your income minus *everything else* has to equal zero.

💳 DEBTS	
Car Payment	$325
Student Loan	$150

EXPENSES	
Saving	$200
Groceries/Restaurants	$300

Updated Totals

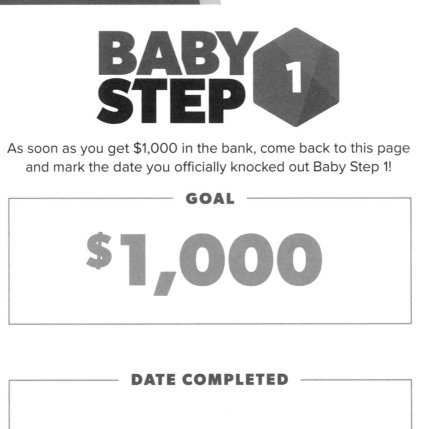

BABY STEP 1

As soon as you get $1,000 in the bank, come back to this page and mark the date you officially knocked out Baby Step 1!

GOAL

$1,000

DATE COMPLETED

_____ / _____ / _____
MONTH   DAY   YEAR

"YOUR *income* IS YOUR MOST **POWERFUL** wealth-building **TOOL.**"

— DAVE RAMSEY

KEY POINTS

Baby Step 2 is paying off all debt (except the house) using the debt snowball.

Debt is not a tool used to build wealth, and payments don't have to be a way of life.

It takes gazelle intensity to get out of debt.

BABY STEP

2

Pay Off All Debt
(Except the House) Using
the Debt Snowball

You've got $1,000 in the bank and you're ready for Baby Step 2: paying off all your debt except your house using the debt snowball! Attack the smallest debt first while making minimum payments on the others. Once you pay off the first one, you'll move to the next smallest debt, taking your freed-up money, newfound motivation, and momentum with you—until you pay off the last, largest debt!

GUIDE
Dave Ramsey

BABY STEP 2

Pay off all _____ (except the house) using the debt snowball.

> **THE RICH RULE OVER THE POOR, AND THE BORROWER IS SLAVE TO THE** *lender.*
>
> PROVERBS 22:7 (NIV)

MYTHS & TRUTHS

MYTH: I need a credit card to rent a car and make purchases online.

TRUTH: You can do both of these things with a _____ card.

. . . .

MYTH: Car payments are a way of life. You can't live without a car payment.

TRUTH: You can stay away from car payments by paying cash for reliable used cars.

Notes _____

_____

_____

MYTH: I need to take out a credit card to build up my credit score.

TRUTH: The FICO score is an "I love _____" score.

....

MYTH: I pay my credit card off every month. And I can earn points and airline miles.

TRUTH: When you use a credit card instead of cash, you actually spend _____ because you don't feel it.

....

MYTH: A credit card is more secure than a debit card.

TRUTH: Debit cards and credit cards have the _____ amount of protection.

....

MYTH: My teenager needs a credit card to learn how to be responsible with money.

TRUTH: More students drop out of school because of _____ trouble than from academic failure.

....

MYTH: Leasing a car is smart. You should always lease things that go down in value. There are tax advantages.

TRUTH: Consumer Reports and a good calculator will tell you that a car _____ is the most expensive way to operate and finance a vehicle.

ANSWER KEY

Debt
More
Same
Financial
Lease

MYTH: I can get a good deal on a new car.

TRUTH: A new car loses _____ of its value in the first five years.

MYTH: A home equity loan is a good option for consolidation and a great substitute for an emergency fund.

TRUTH: You don't go into debt when you're in the middle of an emergency. You'll make the emergency a _____.

MYTH: Debt consolidation is smart. It saves interest and gets you a smaller payment.

TRUTH: Debt consolidation does nothing to change the _____ that got you into debt. So, many actually end up with more debt.

Notes

MYTH: Cosigning a loan is okay if I'm helping a friend or relative.

TRUTH: The bank requires a cosigner because the person isn't likely to _____.

MYTH: You can't go to college without taking out student loans.

TRUTH: _____ of millionaires with a college degree never took out student loans.

BIGGEST MYTH OF ALL

MYTH: Debt is a tool and should be used to create prosperity.

TRUTH: Debt is proof that the borrower is _____ to the lender.

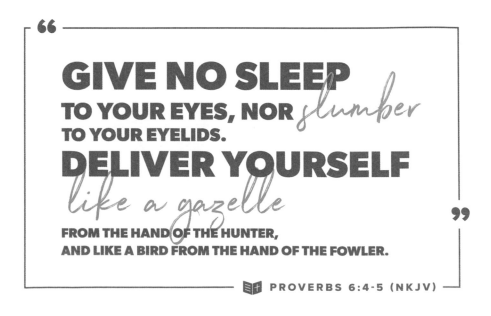

GIVE NO SLEEP TO YOUR EYES, NOR *slumber* TO YOUR EYELIDS. DELIVER YOURSELF *like a gazelle* FROM THE HAND OF THE HUNTER, AND LIKE A BIRD FROM THE HAND OF THE FOWLER.

— PROVERBS 6:4-5 (NKJV)

HOW TO GET OUT OF DEBT

- Quit borrowing more ________________!
- You must ____________ money.
- ____________ something.
- Take a part-time ________.
- ______________ really works.

DEBT SNOWBALL

List your debts smallest to largest. Make minimum payments on all of them and attack the smallest one with a vengeance.

one-minute TAKEAWAY

____

____

____

____

____

____

____

____

ANSWER KEY

Money
Save
Sell
Job
Prayer

IT'S TIME FOR A PLASECTOMY

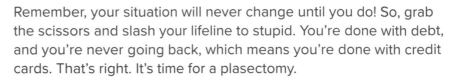

Remember, your situation will never change until you do! So, grab the scissors and slash your lifeline to stupid. You're done with debt, and you're never going back, which means you're done with credit cards. That's right. It's time for a plasectomy.

We get it, this step is hard. But debt has taken too much from you already. And it's the biggest thief of your financial future. So get the cards out of your life and start attacking debt with a vengeance! Goodbye, credit cards. Hello, freedom.

Whether you cut them up in your group or at home on your own, **write down the card information first**! Once you pay them off, you'll have to call and cancel the account.

	CREDIT CARD NAME	PLASECTOMY DATE	CANCEL DATE
1			
2			
3			
4			
5			
6			
7			

HOW TO CLOSE OUT YOUR
CREDIT CARDS

The plasectomy is a mental and physical sign that you're done with debt—forever. *No more. No way. No how.* But there are **three steps** to breaking up with your credit cards for good!

 ## PAY OFF THE BALANCE

Go ahead and cut up the cards. But before you can cancel the accounts, you'll need to pay off the balance. No matter how much you have to pay off, just list the payments in your debt snowball and attack them with gazelle intensity when it's time to pay them off!

2 ## CALL THE CREDIT CARD COMPANY

Once you pay off the balance, call the credit card company and say, "I'm calling to close my account." Spoiler alert: They're going to say whatever they can think of to keep you from leaving. Don't fall for their gimmicks or counter offers. Just repeat, "I'm calling to close my account." Be firm and remember, you're *done* with debt.

3 ## GET IT IN WRITING

When you call to cancel your account, keep a record of the conversation details. You'll want written proof from the company that your account is clear and closed. It's also a good idea to check your credit report later in the year to verify that these accounts are actually closed.

DISCUSSION

Whether you're in a group or online, be honest with your answers and remember to encourage one another!

 1 Look over the list of myths and truths Dave covered in the video. Which myths have fooled you in the past? How can you make sure you don't get duped again?

 2 What fears or concerns do you have about living without credit cards?

 3 Proverbs 22:7 says, " . . . the borrower is slave to the lender" (NIV). What would your life look like if you were totally debt-free? What could you do that you can't afford to do now?

 4 Dave says, "You can wander into debt, but you can't wander out." You'll have to make some tough decisions and sacrifices moving forward. What's one area you can cut back—or cut out—to reach your money goals?

 5 You need serious passion and motivation to get out of debt. What's one thing you can do to kick-start and keep up your gazelle intensity?

KEEP THE CONVERSATION GOING!

Answer these questions online in the Financial Peace community!

financialpeace.com

ACTION STEPS

It's time to live out what you just learned! Complete each of the action steps before the next lesson.

☐ **CUT UP YOUR CREDIT CARDS**
If you didn't do it as part of the activity, gather the family, grab some scissors, and host a plasectomy party! This should be a celebration because it's the moment you decided to stop the crazy cycle of debt. Just remember that cutting up the cards isn't enough. You also need to call each credit card company and close those life-sucking accounts once and for all.

☐ **COMPLETE THE DEBT SNOWBALL**
Enter your debts in your Debt Snowball tool on **financialpeace.com.** The tool will automatically sort your debts from smallest to largest so you can start attacking the smallest debt first. Then set a target date for paying off your last, largest debt! Don't have any debt? Great. You're crushing it. Head to Baby Step 3!

☐ **SELL EVERYTHING IN SIGHT**
That old VCR? *It's out.* The bicycle you haven't ridden in years? *Gone.* Old books, old clothes, old furniture? *Sell. It. All.* Have a garage sale, post everything online—get whatever money you can to knock out your current Baby Step!

☐ **READ *THE DEBT SNOWBALL* ON THE NEXT PAGE**
Need a reminder on how the debt snowball really works? We've got you covered! Check out how this method is the fastest way to get rid of every last debt payment.

THE DEBT *Snowball*

What could you do if you didn't owe anyone your paycheck? That means no student loans, no credit card bills, no car payments—no debt. With the **debt snowball**, you'll pay off the smallest debt first and work your way up to the largest. *But wait.* Doesn't it make sense mathematically to pay off the debt with the highest interest rate first? Maybe. But if you'd been paying attention to math, you wouldn't be in debt. It's time to pay attention to your behavior. Enter the debt snowball.

Attack!

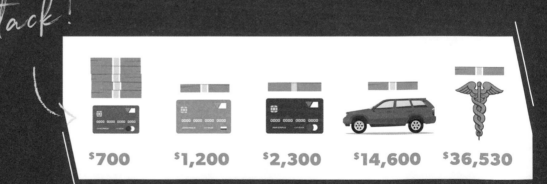

$700 $1,200 $2,300 $14,600 $36,530

1 **LIST YOUR DEBTS FROM SMALLEST TO LARGEST.**
Don't worry about the interest rates! Seriously—smallest to largest.

2 **ATTACK SMALLEST DEBT WITH A VENGEANCE!**
Make minimum payments on all your other debts while you pay off the smallest debt as fast as you can!

3 ## REPEAT THIS METHOD AS YOU PLOW YOUR WAY THROUGH DEBT.

Once that debt is gone, take its payment and apply it to the next smallest debt. The more you pay off, the more your freed-up money grows and gets thrown on the next debt—like a snowball rolling downhill.

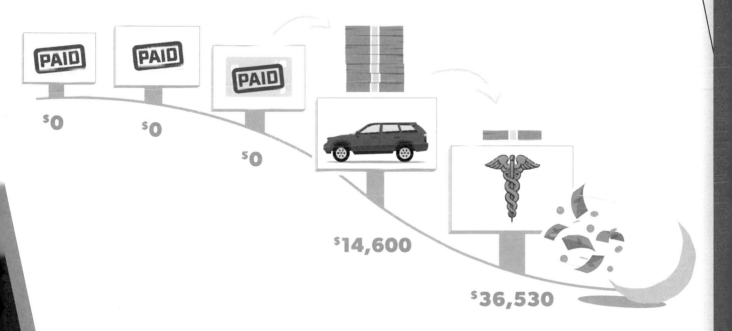

$0 $0 $0 $14,600 $36,530

TRACK YOUR PROGRESS ON FINANCIALPEACE.COM.

Use our Debt Snowball tool to keep up with your attack plan for debt!

BABY STEP 2

Take the total number from your debt snowball and write it below. Then, once you pay off that very last debt, celebrate and come back to this page to mark the day you became debt-free.

GOAL

 $

DATE COMPLETED

_____ / _____ / _____

MONTH   DAY   YEAR

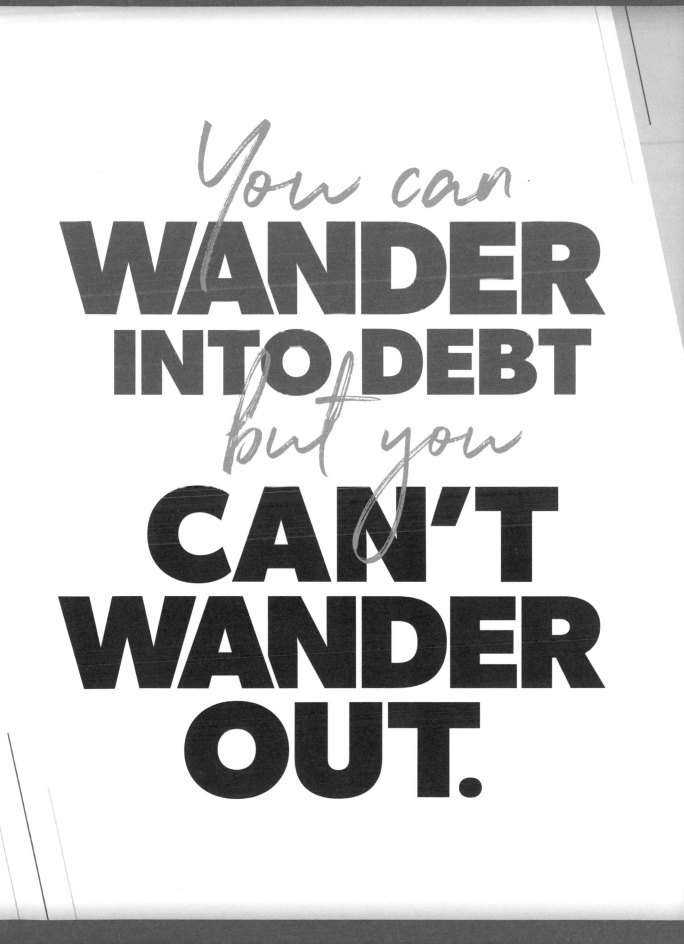

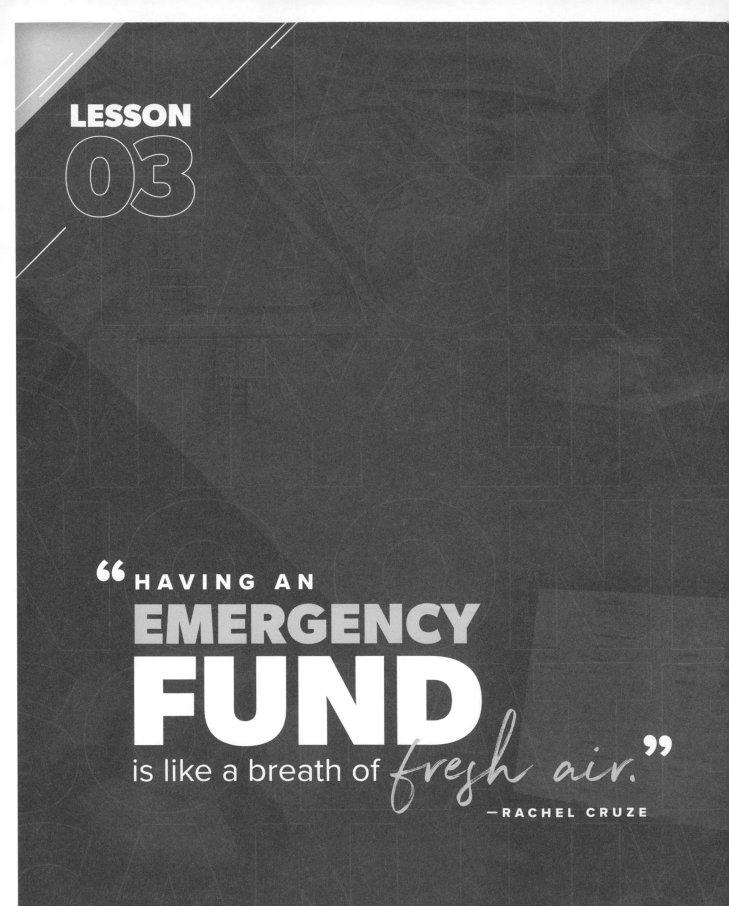

"HAVING AN **EMERGENCY FUND** is like a breath of *fresh air*."

—RACHEL CRUZE

BABY STEP 3

KEY POINTS

Baby Step 3 is saving 3–6 months of expenses in a fully funded emergency fund.

The emergency fund is Murphy repellent. It keeps you from living in fear of the next emergency.

Your emergency fund is insurance, not an investment! It prevents you from going back into debt.

BABY STEP

3

Save 3–6 Months of Expenses in a Fully Funded Emergency Fund

Baby Step 3 is all about building your full emergency fund with 3–6 months of expenses. After the momentum and intensity of Baby Step 2, it's easy to let your foot off the gas. Don't let that happen! Keep your intensity through Baby Step 3. In the same way your $1,000 starter emergency fund kept you from going into debt because of emergency expenses, your fully funded emergency fund will protect you when life's bigger surprises hit.

LESSON 3 //
SAVING

GUIDE
Rachel Cruze

SAVING

"The wise man saves for the future, but the foolish man spends whatever he gets." — PROVERBS 21:20 (TLB)

Nearly 80% of Americans live paycheck to paycheck. They use ___debt___ to cover emergencies.

The emergency fund gives you ___Cash___ to cover emergencies so you stay out of debt.

Notes —————————————————

_____

_____

_____

_____

_____

_____

_____

_____

ANSWER KEY
Debt
Cash

SAVING

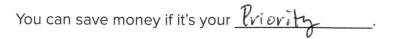

You can save money if it's your ___Priority___.

The ___Cure___ for comparisons is contentment.

___Gratitude___ will lead you to contentment.

> I AM NOT SAYING THIS BECAUSE I AM IN NEED, FOR I HAVE
> **LEARNED TO BE** *content*
> **WHATEVER THE CIRCUMSTANCES.**
>
> PHILIPPIANS 4:11 (NIV)

Notes A heart filled with gratitude leaves no room for discontent.

ANSWER KEY

Priority
Cure
Gratitude

GUIDE
Chris Hogan

BABY STEP 3

Save ___3 – 6 months___ of expenses in a fully funded emergency fund.

Murphy's Law states: Anything that can go wrong ___WILL___ go wrong.

An emergency fund is ___Insurance___. It's not an investment.

When you use it, ___BUILD___ it back up.

> " **AN INTELLIGENT** *heart*
> **ACQUIRES KNOWLEDGE,** "
> **AND THE EAR OF THE WISE SEEKS KNOWLEDGE.**
>
> — PROVERBS 18:15 (ESV)

One-minute TAKEAWAY

Sit down with Thupten & discuss our:
- budget
- flooring plan
- travel saving
- emergency fund (dual)

w/ Yukim & YaYa
- emergency fund ($200)
- watch step 1/2
w/ Yukaiya

ANSWER KEY

3–6 Months
Will
Insurance
Build

STAY GAZELLE *Intense!*

Let's look at two couples. We'll call them **Will & Claire** and **Joe & Kate**.

Both couples were gazelle intense and made extreme sacrifices to pay off their debt. They're finally debt-free! Baby Step 2—check! They take a few weeks to breathe and celebrate before they dive into Baby Step 3.

But now, they're ready to get their **fully funded emergency fund** up and running! They look at their current savings and expenses and decide on their emergency fund goal.

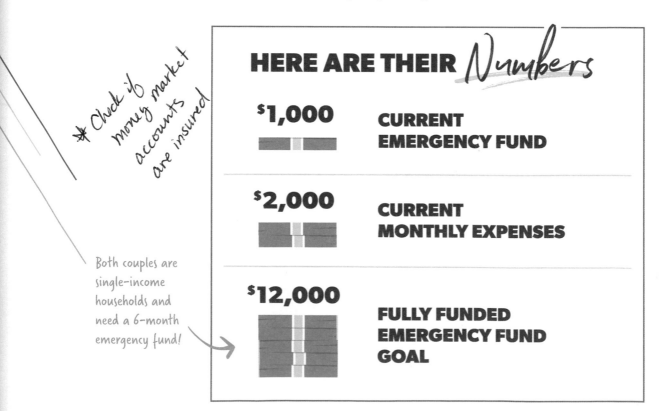

✱ Check if money market accounts are insured

HERE ARE THEIR *Numbers*

$1,000   **CURRENT EMERGENCY FUND**

$2,000   **CURRENT MONTHLY EXPENSES**

Both couples are single-income households and need a 6-month emergency fund!

$12,000   **FULLY FUNDED EMERGENCY FUND GOAL**

HOW TO SAVE FOR BABY STEP 3

With $1,000 already in the bank from Baby Step 1, how many months will it take each couple to reach their $12,000 goal?

WILL & CLAIRE

Will and Claire continue celebrating and let off the gas. They only put **$300 per month** into their emergency fund.

37

MONTHS

JOE & KATE

Joe and Kate stay gazelle intense and put the **$1,000 per month** that *was* going toward debt right into their emergency fund.

11

MONTHS

Moral of the story? **Don't let off the gas!** Take what you were throwing at debt and save it in your fully funded emergency fund. Keep up your gazelle intensity through Baby Step 3!

Respond to the following questions:

 Remember to stay gazelle intense in Baby Step 3. But what's the one way you'll celebrate being debt-free before you kick it back into high gear?

 If these couples asked you about investing or paying off their mortgage before completing Baby Step 3, what advice would you give them? Why?

DISCUSSION

Whether you're in a group or online, be honest with your answers and remember to encourage one another!

 By now, you've seen and experienced the power of the debt snowball. How can its momentum help you knock out your emergency fund? Why is that important to know?

 When have you wished you had Murphy repellent in your life? How would a full emergency fund have turned that crisis into a simple inconvenience?

 In building your emergency fund, consider the suggested savings range of 3–6 months of expenses. Which amount makes the most sense for your life and gives you the most peace?

 Once you're debt-free, it can be tempting to let your foot off the gas and taper off the intensity. But we want you to move through the first three Baby Steps as fast as you can! What are some practical things you can do to maintain your gazelle intensity in Baby Step 3?

KEEP THE CONVERSATION GOING!

Answer these questions online in the Financial Peace community!

financialpeace.com

ACTION STEPS

It's time to live out what you just learned! Complete each of the action steps before the next lesson.

☐ **CALCULATE HOW MUCH YOU NEED FOR** see pg 56
YOUR FULLY FUNDED EMERGENCY FUND
It's time to outwit Murphy! The first step to saving 3–6 months of expenses is figuring out how much you really need. You'll have to answer two questions: How stable or unstable is your income? That helps you determine whether you need closer to three or six months of expenses saved. What are the main expenses in your budget? Crunch some numbers, and you've got a Baby Step 3 goal.

☐ **ROLL THAT SNOWBALL TOWARD BABY STEP 3**
When you reach Baby Step 3, you will have spent months— maybe even years—rolling your debt snowball with gazelle intensity. But now, every cent goes to you, not Sallie Mae or credit card companies. When you're ready for Baby Step 3, create an emergency fund category and just redirect those hard-working snowball dollars right into that fund.

☐ **READ *WHERE TO SAVE BABY STEP 3* ON THE NEXT PAGE**
A money market account is a smart Baby Step 3 choice. Why? These accounts keep your cash safe and accessible. Read on to learn about the account options available to you.

WHERE TO SAVE
BABY STEP 3

You're going to throw all your debt snowball dollars into savings, you've convinced yourself rice and beans aren't *all* that bad, and you promise to keep the second job you're dying to quit—all for Baby Step 3. This is *insurance* after all. This is what will keep you from going back into debt. This is your protection from life's emergencies!

So, how do you keep it safe?

Three words: **money market account.**

Because you need to protect your hard-earned cash (*security*) and still get to it when you need it (*liquidity*), you'll keep your emergency fund in a money market account.

Money market accounts offer security, liquidity, and a *little* bit of interest. It won't earn you much, but we aren't concerned with making money here! Remember, Baby Step 3 is *insurance*, not an investment.

Insurance
—NOT AN INVESTMENT

mutual fund bellwether stock → need more liquidity

THREE OPTIONS WHEN OPENING A MONEY MARKET ACCOUNT:

 LOCAL BANK MONEY MARKET ACCOUNT
Most of these accounts offer higher interest rates for larger balances, along with debit cards or check-writing privileges. Some even let you move money electronically. Finally, bank deposits are insured by the Federal Deposit Insurance Corporation (FDIC) for up to $250,000.

② ONLINE BANK MONEY MARKET ACCOUNT
In general, these types of accounts offer better interest rates and still offer the liquidity and security of a local bank. But like everything else with your money, you need to do plenty of research first. Check out what's available and get what works best for you.

③ MUTUAL FUND MONEY MARKET INVESTMENT ACCOUNT
These accounts might give you a higher return—but there's more risk. Rates can fluctuate, and you may lose money in the short term. While they aren't insured by the FDIC, they are designed to be secure—though you may have more restrictions on using the money.

> **Don't let the options confuse you.** The important thing is to get your money in a secure, accessible account. You're saving up for an inevitable emergency, which means doing nothing is *not* an option. So, do your research, open an account, and keep up your intensity!

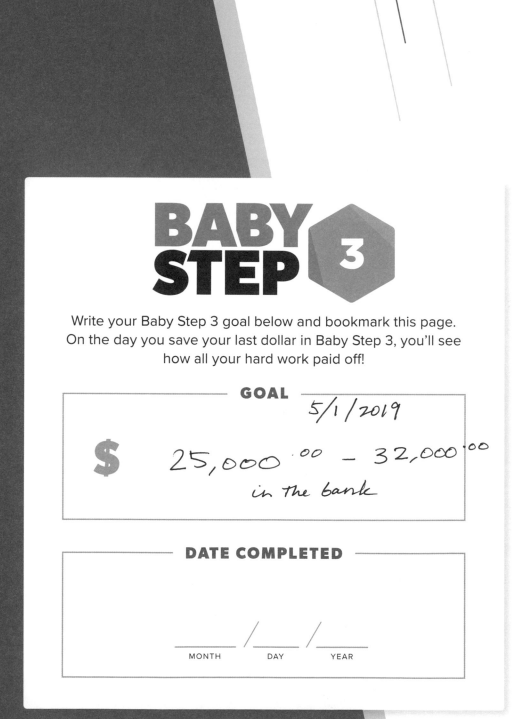

BABY STEP 3

Write your Baby Step 3 goal below and bookmark this page.
On the day you save your last dollar in Baby Step 3, you'll see
how all your hard work paid off!

GOAL

5/1/2019

$ 25,000.00 – 32,000.00
in the bank

DATE COMPLETED

_____ / _____ / _____
MONTH · DAY · YEAR

An Emergency **FUND** **TURNS A** **CRISIS** **INTO** an inconvenience.

LESSON
04

"**INVESTING NOW** WILL *replace* YOUR **PAYCHECK LATER.**"

—CHRIS HOGAN

BABY STEPS 4 5 6 7

KEY POINTS

Baby Step 4 is to invest 15% of your household income in retirement.

Baby Step 5 is to save for your children's college fund.

Baby Step 6 is to pay off your home early.

Baby Step 7 is to build wealth and give.

You'll do Baby Steps 4–6 in order, but at the same time. Then, Baby Step 7 is where you'll have the most fun!

BABY STEP 4

Invest 15% of Your Household Income in Retirement

You've finished paying for the past; now it's time to start paying for your future! On Baby Step 4, you'll invest 15% of your household income into tax-favored accounts for retirement. There is no quick-fix, snap-your-fingers way to build wealth, but you *can* become an everyday millionaire. The key is to start investing early, consistently, and let compound interest work its magic!

GUIDE
Chris Hogan

BABY STEP 4

add 5% gov. match as EXTRA

Invest __15%__ of your household income in retirement.

Investing __$150__ every month from age 25 to 65 (at 11% rate of return) gets you to $1.3 million.

Have a __dream__ __meeting__ with your spouse. If you're single, talk with your accountability partner.

Numbers change when __people__ do.

When you invest 15% of your income every month, you can become an __everyday__ millionaire.

> *Good planning* **AND HARD WORK LEAD TO PROSPERITY, BUT HASTY SHORTCUTS LEAD TO POVERTY.**
>
> 📖 PROVERBS 21:5 (NLT)

Notes

The Story of
JACK & BLAKE
AND THE POWER OF COMPOUND INTEREST

JACK

Jack started investing at the age of 21. He invested $2,400 every year for nine years and then he stopped.

At age 30, Jack put in zero dollars—**zero**! That means *he* stopped but his money *didn't*.

BLAKE

Blake didn't start investing until age 30. He invested $2,400 every year until the age of 67—that's **38 years**!

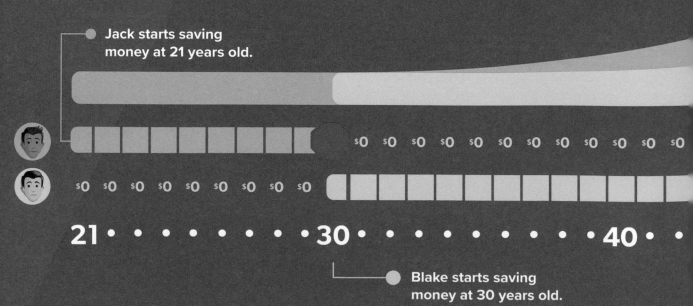

Jack starts saving money at 21 years old.

$0 $0 $0 $0 $0 $0 $0 $0 $0 $0 $0 $0 $0

$0 $0 $0 $0 $0 $0 $0 $0 $0

21 • • • • • • • • **30** • • • • • • • • **40** • •

Blake starts saving money at 30 years old.

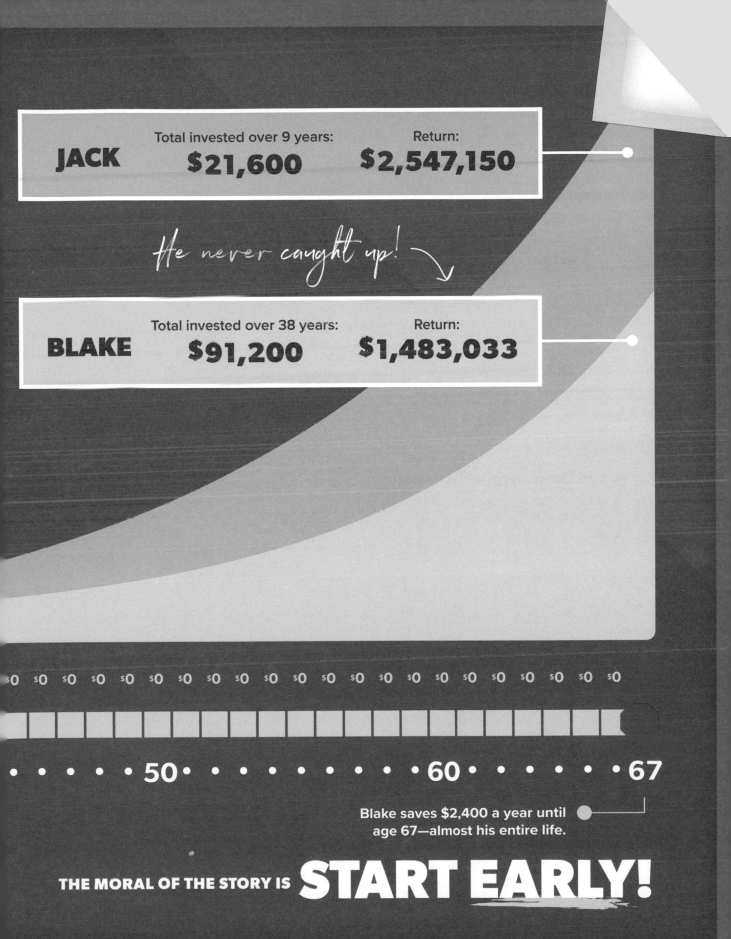

JACK
Total invested over 9 years: **$21,600**
Return: **$2,547,150**

He never caught up!

BLAKE
Total invested over 38 years: **$91,200**
Return: **$1,483,033**

$0 $0 $0 $0 $0 $0 $0 $0 $0 $0 $0 $0 $0 $0 $0 $0 $0 $0 $0 $0 $0 $0

50 **60** **67**

Blake saves $2,400 a year until age 67—almost his entire life.

THE MORAL OF THE STORY IS START EARLY!

BABY STEP

5

Save for Your Children's College Fund

By this step, you've paid off all your debt except the house and you've started saving for retirement. Now it's time to save for your children's college expenses using an Education Savings Account (ESA) or a 529 plan. Help your children go to college the right way—without debt. It *can* be done!

GUIDE
Rachel Cruze

BABY STEP 5

Save for your children's ___College___ fund.

You have two options for college savings—an ___ESA___ and
a ___529___ plan.
• be in control of the money
•

• tax-free
• income limit
• $2000/year

Three ways to go to college debt-free:

1   Select an ___affordable___ school.

2. ___Apply___ for things like scholarships, grants, and
    work study. = FREE MONEY!!

3. Get a ___JOB___.

    10-19hrs/wk = graduate at top
    of class

> ## " COLLEGE IS A BLESSING, NOT AN
> *entitlement.* "
>
> —RACHEL CRUZE

Notes
(15%)
for retirement
the remaining 5% of the 20%
should be used to pay for
school.

BABY STEP

6

Pay Off Your Home Early

Baby Step 6 is the big one! There's only one more thing standing in the way of your complete freedom from debt— your mortgage. This part of paying off debt is a little more like a marathon. But any extra money you can put toward your mortgage will help save you tens of thousands of dollars in interest. And the grass will truly feel different under your feet once it's *yours*.

GUIDE
Dave Ramsey

BABY STEP 6

Pay off your home ___*early*___.

100% of foreclosures occur on a home with

a _____.

Should you PAY OFF YOUR HOME?

INTEREST VS. TAXES

The interest you pay on your mortgage is deductible on your taxes. Are you saving more money by taking this deduction or should you just pay the taxes? Let's take a look.

MORTGAGE INTEREST

deduction

$200K	x	5%	=	$10,000
MORTGAGE AMOUNT		INTEREST RATE		ANNUAL INTEREST PAID

TAXES WITH PAID HOME

married filing jointly at $80k   *or pay tax*

$10K	x	22%	=	$2,200
TAXABLE AMOUNT		TAX BRACKET		TAXES PAID

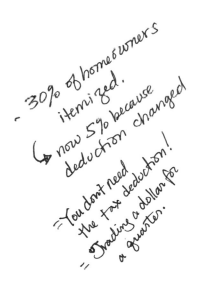

- 30% of homeowners itemized.
  ↳ now 5% because deduction changed
= You don't need the tax deduction!
= Trading a dollar for a quarter.

SO, WHAT MAKES MORE SENSE . . .

PAYING $10,000 TO A BANK OR PAYING $2,200 TO THE IRS?

BABY STEP

7

Build Wealth and Give

You know what people with no debt and no payments can do? Anything they want! Now you can truly live and give like no one else by building wealth, becoming insanely generous, and changing your family tree. Your focus and sacrifice got you here. You made it. You lived like no one else, now you get to *live* and *give* like no one else!

BABY STEP 7

Build wealth and be outrageously _generous_ !

Giving is possibly the most _FUN_ you will ever have with money.

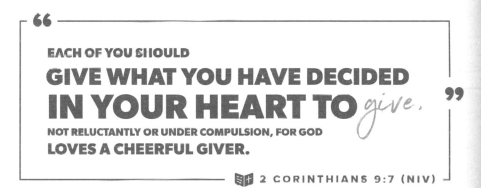

> **EACH OF YOU SHOULD**
> # GIVE WHAT YOU HAVE DECIDED
> # IN YOUR HEART TO *give.*
> **NOT RELUCTANTLY OR UNDER COMPULSION, FOR GOD**
> **LOVES A CHEERFUL GIVER.**
>
> 2 CORINTHIANS 9:7 (NIV)

---

one-minute TAKEAWAY

I MUST utilize the snowball plan and get Thupten on board to pay off his college debt. We will utilize (test) it first by paying off the floors. Knowing that I/we make ENOUGH to be able to

---

Dream FOR YOUR FUTURE

You wake up to silence and sun. There's no alarm clock ringing in your ear. In fact, there's no clock in your bedroom at all. You reach for your phone out of habit and put it back on your nightstand before rolling over in bed. **There's a lot you used to do that you don't have to do anymore.**

You don't check your **inbox**—you couldn't even if you wanted to. You retired years ago, long before your coworkers.

You don't check **social media** when you first wake up. You quit the comparison game back when you learned the power of contentment. Plus, you're living your dream. You don't want someone else's life—you love yours.

You don't check your **bank account**. You know how much you have because you know what you're worth—it's somewhere in the ballpark of seven figures.

You don't check the list of what you must do. You get to list what you want to do. **So, what do you want to do?**

WHAT'S YOUR DREAM RETIREMENT?

Get specific! Want to travel? Write where you want to go. Want to live closer to your kids? Jot down what your dream home looks like. Want to start a business? Put it on paper!

_____

_____

_____

_____

_____

IT'S TIME TO LIVE AND GIVE LIKE NO ONE ELSE.

You're living your dream retirement! You're traveling the way you always wanted. You're spending more time with your kids—and maybe even your grandkids. You own your home—and not just any house on the block, your *dream* home.

You've worked hard for years and years to get to where you are today. And It was *all* worth it.

YOU'RE ON BABY STEP 7!

Now you get to have some serious fun with money.

 You just heard Dave tell the story of his friend who took his entire family on a cruise. **How will you have fun spending your money?**

_____

_____

_____

_____

 You also heard Dave tell the story of this same friend taking his entire family to give bikes away to kids in need. **How will you have fun giving your money?**

_____

_____

_____

_____

_____

DISCUSSION

Whether you're in a group or online, be honest with your answers and remember to encourage one another!

 What has been your plan for retirement up to this point? How has this lesson changed the way you think about saving for and dreaming about retirement?

 If you're a parent, how do you feel about investing for retirement before saving for your children's college fund? Based on the ages of your kids, what is your plan to send them to college debt-free?

 If you're currently paying a mortgage each month, how would paying off your home early change your life? What would you be able to do that you can't do now?

 When is a time that generosity has impacted your life? Were you the giver or the receiver?

KEEP THE CONVERSATION GOING!

Answer these questions online in the Financial Peace community!

financialpeace.com

ACTION STEPS

It's time to live out what you just learned! Complete each of the action steps before the next lesson.

☐ **SCHEDULE A BUDGET COMMITTEE MEETING**
You're coming up on your next budgeting cycle! Remember, it takes about three months to get the budget right, so don't get frustrated. If you're married, schedule your next Budget Committee Meeting. Singles, don't forget to review your budget with your accountability partner.

☐ **MAKE SURE GIVING IS AT THE TOP OF YOUR BUDGET**
When you hold money with an open hand—not a clenched fist—you're able to give generously *and* receive graciously. No matter which Baby Step you're on, giving is your priority whether that's a tithe to your church or contributions to charity.

☐ **CONTACT A SMARTVESTOR PRO**
If you're ready for Baby Step 4, check out our list of SmartVestor Pros near you at **financialpeace.com**. These investing professionals will help you invest the right way!

☐ **RESEARCH ESAS OR 529 PLANS AND SCHOLARSHIPS**
You can also connect with a SmartVestor Pro to start an Education Savings Account (ESA) or 529 plan. If your teen is closer to college, help them find scholarships to apply for instead. Remember, debt-free college is the *only* option!

☐ **READ *IN ORDER, BUT AT THE SAME TIME* ON THE NEXT PAGE**
The Baby Steps work when you do them in order. But Baby Steps 4–6 are done at the same time! We know that sounds confusing, but this deep dive tells you exactly what we mean.

BABY STEPS  4 5 6

IN ORDER, BUT AT THE SAME TIME

You do Baby Steps 1, 2, and 3 one at a time. Check. You do Baby Steps 4, 5, and 6 at the same time. *What?*

Baby Steps 1, 2, and 3 require laser focus and gazelle intensity—and they each have a specific dollar goal. After Baby Step 3, however, the plan changes gears. You'll do Steps 4, 5, and 6 in order, but at the same time.

Here's what we mean:

Meet the Campbells.

This average American family has a household income of $5,000 per month. They used the debt snowball to send $1,500 per month to pay off all their debt. Then they used the *same* gazelle intensity and saved $1,500 per month to finish their emergency fund.

The Campbells celebrate! They get to ease up on their intensity some, but they're ready to attack **Baby Steps 4, 5, and 6—in order, but at the same time**.

IF THEY SET ASIDE $1,000 FOR THESE BABY STEPS, WATCH WHAT WOULD HAPPEN:

 1 **START BABY STEP 4**

The Campbells save 15% of their gross income in retirement. So, they open a Roth 401(k) and start investing $750 every month.

4 Roth 401(k): **$750**

$250 left to budget

---

2 **START BABY STEP 5**

They open an ESA for their 3-year-old and contribute $166 per month. (That's the ESA contribution limit as of 2018.)

4 Roth 401(k): **$750**   **5** ESA: **$166**

$84 left to budget

---

3 **START BABY STEP 6**

The Campbells still have $84! They go ahead and add it to their mortgage payment knowing they could find more money in the budget to throw at their home if they wanted to.

4 Roth 401(k): **$750**   **5** ESA: **$166**   **6** Extra on home: **$84**

$0 left to budget!

There you have it. Baby Steps 4, 5, and 6—**IN ORDER, BUT AT THE SAME TIME.**

"IN A *heart* FILLED WITH GRATITUDE THERE IS NO ROOM FOR DISCONTENTMENT."

—RACHEL CRUZE

BUYER BEWARE

KEY POINTS

There are a million marketing tactics trying to get at your money and bust your budget.

You *can* have power over your purchases.

Contentment keeps your stuff from owning you.

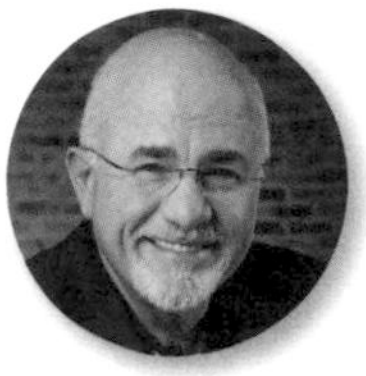

GUIDE
Dave Ramsey

CAVEAT EMPTOR

Companies use every angle to aggressively compete for your money.

We live in the most marketed-to culture in the history of the world.

MAJOR WAYS COMPANIES MARKET TO US

1. Personal Selling (one-on-one)
2. financing and convenient payment methods as a marketing tool
3. TV, radio, magazines, internet and other media
4. Product positioning
   - Brand Recognition
   - Color
   - Shelf Position and Packaging

You don't FEEL financing.

Don't be led to the slaughter!

SIGNIFICANT PURCHASES

A "significant purchase" is normally anything over $300.

Our bodies go through physiological changes when making a significant purchase.

ANSWER KEY

Money
Most
Personal
Financing
Convenient
Internet
Positioning
$300
Changes

folly = fool in action

POWER OVER PURCHASE

- Wait _overnight_ before making a purchase.
- Carefully consider your buying _motives_ (*need or want?*)
- Never buy anything that you do not _understand_.
- Consider the "_opportunity_ cost" of your money.
- Seek the _Counsel_ of your spouse.

Cheater!!

" QUIT CHASING HAPPINESS

with stuff. "

—DAVE RAMSEY

Notes Any financial decisions, whether big or small, should be discussed.

GUIDE
Rachel Cruze

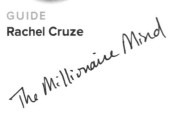

The Millionaire Mind

7 TIPS FOR NEGOTIATING

1. Always tell the absolute ___truth___.

2. Use the power of ___cash___. *= no loans or checks to deal with for the seller.*

3. Understand and use ___walk___ - ___away___ power.

4. Learn to ___shut___ ___up___.

5. Say, "That's not good ___enough___!"

6. Identify the ___good___ guy, ___bad___ guy technique.

7. Master the "if I ___take___ away" technique.

⏱ one-minute TAKEAWAY

NEED TO HAVE THURPTEN INVOLVED IN BUDGET DECISIONS !!

WHAT TO DO:

If you've ever messed up the budget, you probably overspent on wants by convincing yourself they were needs. In the quiz, mark each item as a want or a need. If you're married, discuss the items where you and your spouse disagree.

NEEDS & WANTS QUIZ

	Need	Want
Movie/TV streaming subscription		✓
Groceries	✓	
New shoes		✓
A place to live	✓	
Another car		✓
Utilities: electricity, gas, water, etc.	✓	
New clothes		✓
A cruise vacation		✓
Lawn care service		✓
Car wash		✓
Childcare/day care	✓	
Going out to eat everyday		✓
Concert or game tickets		✓
Auto insurance	✓	
Newest cell phone available		✓
Premium pet food		✓
Current cell phone plan	✓	
Gym membership		✓

Respond to the following questions:

 1. What is one item on this list that you thought was a need, but is actually a want?   *Cell phone plan*

 2. How does identifying something as a want versus a need change your spending habits?   *Makes you think about your MOTIVES.*

Wants = Budget Breaker!!
Needs = rarely breaks a budget.

DISCUSSION

Whether you're in a group or online, be honest with your answers and remember to encourage one another!

 1 When was the last time you bought something because of a compelling ad on TV or social media? What about the ad made you dip into your wallet?

 2 What's the danger of not talking with your spouse before making a major purchase?

 3 What's the worst impulse purchase you've ever made? Why was it so bad? How would you do things differently next time?

 4 Think about the idea of opportunity cost: *If I spend money on this, then I can't spend it on that.* How does opportunity cost help you prioritize your spending?

 5 On a scale of 1–10, with 1 being "terrified" and 10 being "energized," how would you rank your feelings about negotiating? Why?

KEEP THE CONVERSATION GOING!

Answer these questions online in the Financial Peace community!

financialpeace.com

ACTION STEP

It's time to live out what you just learned! Comple
action steps before the next lesson.

☐ **DEFINE YOUR MAJOR PURCHASES**
What's a "major purchase" in your world? Put a number to it!
Singles, run this by your accountability partner to get their
feedback. Married couples, decide on this number together.

☐ **GET A BETTER DEAL**
Don't just settle for regular retail outlets. Get creative and find
some places where you could get the same thing cheaper:
flea market, discount store, scratch/dent store, or resale shop.
Identify five things you regularly purchase. How could you find
them cheaper?

☐ **SET SOCIAL MEDIA LIMITS**
Wise spending has a lot to do with contentment, and
contentment can have a lot to do with what you see on social
media. This week, take some practical steps toward limiting
social media's negative impact. Try to avoid social media when
you first wake up and choose one day to *completely* unplug.

☐ **READ *NEGOTIATE A WIN-WIN* ON THE NEXT PAGE**
If you've never tried to wheel and deal before, negotiating
can seem intimidating—but it doesn't have to be! Now that
you're armed with our seven negotiating tips, read on for the
confidence boost you need to get the deal you want.

NEGOTIATE
A WIN-WIN

Everybody wants to get a good deal. That's the happy ending to the spending story, right?

But it can be hard when it seems like everyone is trying to sell you something, and they're just out to get your money. So how can you get the things you need, the things you really want, and still stay on track and on budget?

You negotiate.

If you're immediately intimidated or offended by that word, check out this negotiation story from one of our *Financial Peace University* members! She hits at least four of the seven tips Rachel talks about.

BETHANY WHEELS AND DEALS

For the past several years, my jobs had always included a company car. When we decided to move to Nashville, that meant giving up the company car and getting my own—super intimidating since neither my husband nor I had ever negotiated anything, let alone a car.

USE THE POWER OF CASH.

We had saved up money to pay cash for the car and our budget was around $10,000. We went to a local car lot (known for great prices and quality cars) and were immediately approached by a salesperson who asked us what we wanted and what our budget was. We hadn't looked at any particular cars before we got there so we were open to most anything.

UNDERSTAND WALK-AWAY POWER.

We weren't jazzed about anything on the lot, and then I eyed a black SUV that was listed at $12,500—clearly over budget. I test-drove it and loved it but tried my best not to get too excited. The biggest key to negotiating is being content to walk away.

IDENTIFY THE GOOD GUY, BAD GUY TECHNIQUE.

We noticed that the tires were going to need to be replaced soon, and it would need the usual 100,000-mile maintenance. With that in mind, we lowballed and made an offer of $7,500—in cash. The salesperson was "on our side" but said he couldn't take that offer to the manager.

SAY, "THAT'S NOT GOOD ENOUGH!"

We came up to $8,000 and the manager offered to give it to us for $12,000 if we financed—big nope. We reiterated that we were paying cash and told them the $500 off wasn't good enough. After a couple more go-rounds, we made a final offer of $9,800, fees and licensing included.

USE WALK-AWAY POWER.

He said no, so we thanked him, and with a little grit, walked away. As we were approaching our car, the manager ran out and we hear, "$10,000 if you finance!"

We were mainly just annoyed at that point, so we had no trouble driving away in the car we showed up in.

We let it go and planned on going to another lot once we moved. But we got a text the next morning from the salesperson asking us to come back. They offered us $9,100 plus licensing and fees. We accepted. Total cost: $10,101. BOOM!

We wrote the check, drove it off the lot, and moved to Nashville the next morning. And that's what we call the power of negotiation.

— BETHANY 99

Score a deal!

You may not always get a bargain like Bethany. Sometimes, the seller won't budge. Sometimes, when you walk away, the seller will let you. But most times, if you want to negotiate, the seller is willing! Because when you buy a *deal* and they leave with a *sale*, that's what we call a **win-win**.

LESSON
06

" INSURANCE
PROTECTS
the things that will
MAKE YOU *wealthy.* "

—DAVE RAMSEY

THE ROLE OF INSURANCE

KEY POINTS

The purpose of insurance is simply to transfer risk—this is your defensive game plan.

There are seven basic insurances you actually need.

No exceptions and no excuses, everyone eighteen and older needs a written will.

GUIDE
Dave Ramsey

AUTO INSURANCE

If you have a full emergency fund, raise

your _____.

Carry adequate _____.

Consider dropping your _____ on older cars.

HOMEOWNER'S AND RENTER'S INSURANCE

Homeowner's coverage should be guaranteed

_____ cost if at all possible.

If you're in an apartment or other rental arrangement, you

need _____ insurance.

An _____ liability policy is a good buy once

you begin building wealth.

" **THE PURPOSE OF INSURANCE IS**
to transfer risk. "

–DAVE RAMSEY

HEALTH INSURANCE

Increase your deductible and/or coinsurance amount to bring ________________ down.

Increase your ____________-____________ but never decrease the ________________ pay.

The HSA (Health Savings Account) is a ______-________________ savings account for medical expenses that works with a high-deductible insurance policy.

Notes

ANSWER KEY

Premiums
Stop-Loss
Maximum
Tax-Sheltered

DISABILITY INSURANCE

Disability is designed to replace lost _____ due to a short-term or permanent disability.

Try to buy disability insurance that pays if you cannot perform the job that you were educated or trained to do. That is called _____, or "own occ," disability.

Beware of _____-term policies covering less than five years.

Your coverage should be for _____ of your current income.

A _____ elimination period will _____ your premium cost.

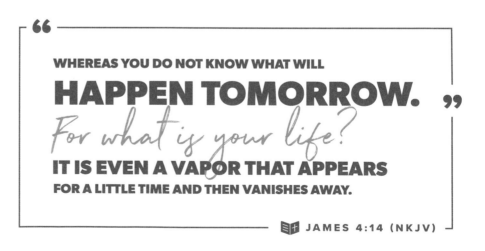

WHEREAS YOU DO NOT KNOW WHAT WILL

HAPPEN TOMORROW. "

For what is your life?

IT IS EVEN A VAPOR THAT APPEARS

FOR A LITTLE TIME AND THEN VANISHES AWAY.

JAMES 4:14 (NKJV)

ANSWER KEY

Income
Occupational
Short
65%
Longer
Lower

LONG-TERM CARE INSURANCE

Long-term care insurance is for _____ home,

assisted living facilities, and in-home care.

This is a must-have for anyone _____ years old or older.

IDENTITY THEFT PROTECTION

Don't buy ID theft protection that only provides credit

report _____.

Good protection includes _____ services

that assign a counselor to clean up the mess.

Notes

LIFE INSURANCE

Life insurance is to replace lost income due to _____.

_____ insurance is for a specified period, is substantially cheaper, and has no savings plan built into it.

_____ _____ insurance is normally for life and is more expensive in order to fund a savings plan.

You need about _____ times your income. Invested at a 10–12% rate of return, the growth would replace your lost income.

Don't forget your _____.

Children only need enough for _____ expenses.

Notes _____

_____

_____

_____

_____

_____

ANSWER KEY

Death
Term
Cash Value
10
Spouse
Burial

" NEVER DO INVESTMENT-TYPE *insurance.* "

—DAVE RAMSEY

INSURANCE TO AVOID

- Credit life and disability

- Cancer and hospital indemnity

- Accidental death

- Prepaid burial policies

- Mortgage life insurance

- Policies with fancy options: return of premium
  and waiver of premium

Get a written _____.

one-minute TAKEAWAY

_____

_____

_____

_____

_____

ANSWER KEY

Will

BUY THE RIGHT *Coverage*

AUTO INSURANCE POLICY

Whether you drive a nice car or a beater, you want to make sure you're covered in case life decides to hit you . . . or your car. This is not the time to go cheap on your insurance policy! Work through Luke's scenario to find out why.

Luke's working the Baby Steps and wants to save money wherever he can. So, he gets the state minimum 25/50/15 liability policy.

25   50   15

COVERS INJURIES TO INDIVIDUALS

The maximum amount (in thousands of dollars) **per person** that will be covered

COVERS THE TOTAL OF ALL INJURIES TO PEOPLE

The maximum amount (in thousands of dollars) **per accident** that will be covered

COVERS DAMAGE TO PROPERTY

The maximum amount (in thousands of dollars) **per accident** that will be covered

ON HIS WAY TO WORK, LUKE HITS A CAR.

The driver of the other car experiences **$30,000** in injury costs and the passenger experiences **$75,000** in injury costs. Luke totals his car and the **$50,000** car of the other driver. Determine how much Luke will have to pay *after* his insurance pays their portion for each of the following.

25/50/15	DRIVER	PASSENGER	DRIVER'S CAR
TOTAL COST OF ACCIDENT	$ 30,000	$ 75,000	$ 50,000
25/50/15 INSURANCE PAYS	− $ 25,000	− $ 25,000	− $ 15,000
LUKE PAYS	= $ 5,000	= $ 50,000	= $ 35,000

Maxes at $50k

LUKE HAS TO PAY: $ _____

And this doesn't even include the cost to replace his own car!

Now, work the same scenario, but this time Luke has a good **100/300/100** insurance policy.

100/300/100	DRIVER	PASSENGER	DRIVER'S CAR
TOTAL COST OF ACCIDENT	$ 30,000	$ 75,000	$ 50,000
100/300/100 INSURANCE PAYS	− $ _____	− $ _____	− $ _____
LUKE PAYS	= $ _____	= $ _____	= $ _____

Maxes at $300k

LUKE HAS TO PAY: $ _____

(of course, he still has to replace his own car.)

Respond to the following questions:

1. Was the cheaper liability policy (25/50/15) a good choice for Luke? Why or why not?

DISCUSSION

Whether you're in a group or online, be honest with your answers and remember to encourage one another!

 When have you let the *cost* of insurance dictate how *much* insurance you get in a certain policy? How does this lesson challenge you to think differently?

 How do you see your fully funded emergency fund fitting into your insurance plan? How can you make sure you have the right balance between the two?

 Everyone eighteen and over needs a will. Do you have a will? If not, what has been holding you back from getting one?

 Can you imagine building wealth to the point where you can self-insure? Why or why not? How have the Baby Steps moved you closer to making that a reality?

**KEEP THE
CONVERSATION
GOING!**

Answer these questions online in the Financial Peace community!

financialpeace.com

ACTION STEPS

It's time to live out what you just learned! Complete each of the action steps before the next lesson.

☐ **EVALUATE YOUR CURRENT INSURANCE PLAN**
Use the Coverage Checkup tool on **financialpeace.com** to figure out what you need (and don't need), which questions to ask, and where to get the best coverage.

☐ **GET A WILL**
This is pretty simple. If you are eighteen or older, you need a will. Get it done—no exceptions, no excuses. It's one of the best gifts you can give your family!

☐ **LOOK INTO GETTING AN HSA**
A good Health Savings Account (HSA) can become a "medical envelope" for you and your family. But you need to do a little research to make sure it fits your situation. Talk with your employer about what your company might offer.

☐ **READ *TERM LIFE INSURANCE—THE WAY TO GO* ON THE NEXT PAGE**
You know we're not too big on whole life insurance. In fact, we hate it. But we do recommend you get term life insurance. Read on to learn what you need and why!

Term Life INSURANCE
———————— THE WAY TO GO

Life happens, and without being too morbid, so does unexpected death. We want you to have peace of mind knowing your family will be taken care of when you're gone.

It doesn't matter if you're newly married or heading into retirement. If someone depends on your income, you need life insurance. Plain and simple.

WHOLE LIFE *vs.* TERM LIFE INSURANCE

There are several types of life insurance—term, whole life, or any kind of cash value life insurance. Term is straightforward, inexpensive, and protects your family. The other ones? Total rip-offs.

 Whole life insurance often costs hundreds of dollars more a month and includes a "savings" plan with a terrible return. Instead, opt for term life. You'll pay a fraction of the price, then just invest the difference in what you would have paid for whole life insurance.

 Term life insurance is the easiest and least expensive way to protect your family's finances after you're gone. Simply put, here's how term life insurance works: if you or your spouse passes away at any time during this term, your beneficiaries will receive a payout from the policy.

HOW LONG DO I NEED COVERAGE?

Dave's general rule is to buy based on when your kids will be heading off to college and living on their own. Typical terms are 10, 15, 20, or 30 years. **We recommend a 15- or 20-year term.**

Have a newborn in the house? Pick up a 20-year plan. If you have a ten-year-old, a 15-year plan would be a better option for you.

HOW MUCH COVERAGE DO I NEED?

That small policy you're getting through work, which might be one year's worth of coverage, isn't near enough. Always buy a policy that covers **ten to twelve times your annual pretax income.**

With a good term life policy, by investing the insurance proceeds, your beneficiaries can earn a rate of return that replaces your lost earnings and provides security for your family after you're gone.

Here's what we mean. Let's say you make $40,000. That means you should carry at least $400,000 in coverage.

If your surviving spouse invests that $400,000 in good mutual funds with an average 11% return, they could peel off $44,000 a year from that investment to replace your income without ever cutting into the original investment amount. That's what we call real security.

Get the Right Coverage Today

Simply put, life insurance has one job: it replaces your income when you die.

We hope you'll never have to use it, but the truth is we can't see the future and we aren't promised tomorrow. So the ideal time to buy life insurance is today! Use the **Coverage Checkup tool on financialpeace.com** to get the best term life insurance policy for your family.

" **GOALS** are *dreams* with **WORK BOOTS ON.** "

—DAVE RAMSEY

RETIREMENT PLANNING

KEY POINTS

Investing doesn't have to be complicated. Use the KISS rule: Keep It Simple, Stupid.

Never invest in things you don't understand.

The best way to build wealth is slowly and consistently over time.

GUIDE
Dave Ramsey

GROUND RULES FOR INVESTING

Baby Step 4 is to invest _____ of your household income into Roth IRAs and pretax retirement plans.

The KISS Rule of Investing: Keep it _____, stupid.

Diversification _____ risk.

> **INVEST IN SEVEN VENTURES, YES, IN EIGHT;**
> ## YOU DO NOT KNOW
> **WHAT DISASTER MAY COME UPON** *the land.* "
>
> 📖 **ECCLESIASTES 11:2 (NIV)**

MUTUAL FUNDS

_____ _____ are where investors pool their money to invest.

Your return comes as the _____ of the fund is increased.

Mutual funds are good for _____-_____ investments.

ANSWER KEY

15%
Simple
Lowers
Mutual Funds
Value
Long-Term

///

USE TAX-FAVORED PLANS

Tax-favored means the investment is in

a _____ _____ or has a

special tax treatment.

Roth = after tax

Oregon = 9-11% tax

QUALIFIED PLANS

- Individual Retirement Arrangement (IRA)
- 401(k)
- 403(b)
- 457
- Simplified Employee Pension Plan

Notes _____

_____

_____

_____

_____

_____

_____

_____

ANSWER KEY

Qualified Plan

INDIVIDUAL RETIREMENT ARRANGEMENT (IRA)

Remember, an IRA is the tax _____ on virtually any type of investment. It is *not* a type of investment at a bank.

ROTH IRA

The Roth IRA is an after-tax IRA that grows tax-_____.

> ## " IF YOU WANT TO BE A MILLIONAIRE, FIGURE OUT WHAT MILLIONAIRES DO AND START DOING IT.
> *Then you'll get to be one.* "
>
> —DAVE RAMSEY

401(K), 403(B), AND 457 RETIREMENT PLANS

Some companies are now offering the _____ 401(k), which grows tax-free.

You should be funding your plan whether your company _____ or not, but the plans that have company matching provide great returns.

ROLLOVERS

You should ______________ roll all retirement plans to an IRA when you leave a company.

Don't bring the money home! Make it a ______________ transfer.

RETIREMENT LOANS

Never ______________ on your retirement plan.

Notes

ANSWER KEY

Always
Direct
Borrow

OUR SUGGESTION FOR INVESTING 15%

Fund a 401(k) of other employer plans if they match. Fund an amount ______________ to the match.

Above the match amount, fund ______________ IRAs. If there is no match, start with Roth IRAs.

Complete the 15% of your income by going back to the ______________ or other company plans.

BUILDING WEALTH

The ________________ wins every time.

So, 15% of your income going into retirement isn't for one month or one year. It's for the rest of your ___________.

one-minute TAKEAWAY

____

____

____

____

____

ANSWER KEY

Equal
Roth
401(k)
Tortoise
Life

WHAT COULD YOUR MONEY *Turn Into?*

Your most powerful wealth-building tool is your income until your investments start earning more than you do. That's why you want to get to **Baby Step 4** as fast as you can!

Take your current monthly gross income and calculate how much you would invest if you were on Baby Step 4.

ON BABY STEP 4, I WOULD NEED TO INVEST:

$ _____   x   **15%**   =   _____
MONTHLY GROSS INCOME   PERCENT   MONTHLY CONTRIBUTION

Before the next lesson, you'll go to **financialpeace.com** and use the Investment Calculator to see exactly what your monthly investment could look like in **20, 30, and 40 years** at an 11% rate of return!

For now, check out the table below to get ballpark numbers.

MONTHLY CONTRIBUTION	20 YEARS	30 YEARS	40 YEARS
$700	$611,501	$1,981,159	$6,075,272
$800	$698,858	$2,264,182	$6,943,168
$900	$786,215	$2,547,205	$7,811,067

Respond to the following questions:

 What comes to mind when you see what your monthly investment could turn into?

 How do you feel knowing that if your income increases, you'll get to invest even *more* each month?

DISCUSSION

Whether you're in a group or online, be honest with your answers and remember to encourage one another!

 1 If the stock market goes up, keep investing. If the stock market goes down, guess what? You keep investing! Dave says the only people who get hurt on a roller coaster are the ones who try to jump off midway. What has always made you nervous about investing? How has what you learned in this lesson calmed some of those fears?

 2 What are some of the big problems with investments like gold, certificates of deposits, single stocks, and bonds? What should you do if you're investing in them right now?

 3 Investing is the key to building wealth, and building wealth is the key to creating a legacy that will outlive you. How do you want to set your family up for success after you're gone?

 4 Right now, are you the tortoise or the hare? What should you be doing to make sure you always win with investing?

**KEEP THE
CONVERSATION
GOING!**

Answer these questions online in the Financial Peace community!

financialpeace.com

ACTION STEPS

It's time to live out what you just learned! Complete each of the action steps before the next lesson.

☐ **USE THE INVESTMENT CALCULATOR**
In the activity, you calculated 15% of your monthly income that will go into retirement savings. Ready to see what that number could become in 20, 30, and 40 years? Use the Investment Calculator at **financialpeace.com** to see what your monthly investment could turn into!

☐ **SPREAD THAT MONEY AROUND**
In this lesson, you learned about diversification—spreading money around so it will grow. You want to keep your risk low and your reward high! If you're ready for Baby Step 4, go to **financialpeace.com** to connect with a SmartVestor Pro in your area and start investing the right way.

☐ **CHECK YOUR GAZELLE INTENSITY**
You're seven lessons into *Financial Peace University*, and you're doing great. How are you feeling about your progress? Use the scale below to gauge your gazelle intensity.

| 1 | 2 | 3 | 4 | 5 | 6 | 7 | 8 | 9 | 10 |

← **RUNNING SLOW**   **STARVING THE CHEETAH!**

If you're at a 10, great work! If you're running a little slow, what's one thing you can do this week to amp up your intensity?

☐ **READ *MUTUAL FUNDS 101* ON THE NEXT PAGE**
Investing isn't one size fits all. Because you never invest in something you don't understand, you need to learn what's best for you. Read on for a crash course on mutual funds!

MUTUAL FUNDS 101

If you want to win with money, find someone who's won with money and copy them. If you want to build wealth, find someone who's wealthy and copy them! The good news is we found 10,000 of them for you.

In our research for Chris Hogan's book *Everyday Millionaires: How Ordinary People Built Extraordinary Wealth—and How You Can Too*, we surveyed over 10,000 millionaires and asked them how they built their wealth. The number one answer? By investing early and consistently in their company 401(k) plans.

That's why we do **Baby Step 4**: Invest 15% of your household income in retirement.

When you're ready to start investing, you won't need to camp out on the trading floor of the New York Stock Exchange. Just keep it simple and follow the investing advice that's worked for over 20 years!

Invest in the right mix of **mutual funds** with a history of strong performance and stick with them over time.

THE 4 TYPES OF MUTUAL FUNDS
You Should Use!

GROWTH

Growth funds are some of the most common types of mutual funds. Using mid-cap funds (cap is short for capitalization, or money), they generally include medium-sized companies that are still growing—and still making money. Growth funds can provide above-average growth for your money with above-average risk. Over the long run though, they live up to their name: growth funds.

GROWTH AND INCOME

Dave calls these "obedient, predictable child" funds. They include large-cap funds with a lot of big-name companies you probably recognize. Growth and income funds usually grow steadily with an average risk. So, you won't make a fortune overnight, but you won't lose it all either.

AGGRESSIVE GROWTH

Dave calls these "wild child" funds. They can have an incredible return one year, then lose money the next. A small-cap fund is one example of an aggressive growth fund. These funds are generally made up of smaller, active, emerging companies, such as start-ups and tech companies. They have the potential for a higher return—but also carry greater risk.

INTERNATIONAL

International funds invest in companies outside the United States. But they still might be companies you recognize. That's because so many products created in the United States are actually owned by international companies. International funds carry varying degrees of risk, but they're great for diversification.

Let us help!

Investing doesn't have to be intimidating. A SmartVestor Pro can help you invest the right way. Find these investing professionals in your local area at **financialpeace.com**.

"THE GRASS
AT YOUR HOUSE
FEELS DIFFERENT
WHEN YOU *own it.*"

—DAVE RAMSEY

REAL ESTATE & MORTGAGES

KEY POINTS

A house is the largest financial investment you will ever make.

Here's your home-buying plan: a 15-year fixed-rate mortgage with at least a 10% down payment, and monthly payments of no more than 25% of your take-home pay.

When you pay off your home, you're 100% debt-free!

GUIDE
Dave Ramsey

RENTING

There is nothing wrong with _____ for a little while. This demonstrates patience and wisdom. *I year of Marriage to know how close to your in-laws to buy.*

WHEN TO BUY

You should be finished with Baby Step 3. That means you are debt-free and have a full emergency fund in place.

WHY TO BUY

- It's a ___*forced*___ savings plan.
- It's an ___*inflation*___ hedge.
- It grows virtually ___TAX___ - ___FREE___.

Notes _____

_____

_____

_____

_____

_____

_____

//.

WHAT TO BUY

- Buy in the __bottom__ price range of the neighborhood, and never overbuild your neighborhood through home additions and improvements.

- Homes appreciate in good neighborhoods and are priced based on three things: location, location, and location.

- If possible, buy near water or with a __view__.

- Buy bargains by overlooking bad landscaping, ugly carpet, outdated wallpaper, and the Elvis print in the master bedroom.

- Always buy a home that is (or can be) attractive from the street and has a good basic floor plan.

Notes

GUIDE
Chris Hogan

HOW TO BUY

Real estate agents have full access to the _Multiple_ Listing Service (MLS) and can make house hunting easier.

* Always get a land survey if you're buying more than a standard subdivision lot.

Have the home inspected mechanically and structurally by a certified _home inspector_. Get an appraisal but understand that it's just an "opinion of value."

* Title insurance insures you against an unclean title, which is when your property ownership is called into question. It is a must buy.

Get a monthly payment of no more than _25%_ of your take-home pay on a _15-year_ fixed-rate loan, with at least _10%_ down.

> "
> **AS FOR ME**
> **AND MY HOUSE,**
> **WE WILL SERVE** *the Lord.*
> "
>
> — JOSHUA 24:15 (ESV)

///.

HORRIBLE MORTGAGE OPTIONS

- <u>ARMs</u> or Adjustable-Rate Mortgages

  o The concept of the ARM is to transfer the risk of higher interest rates to the borrower. So, in return, the lender gives a lower rate.

  o If you have an ARM, refinance immediately!

- Interest-only loans are a bad idea because you're only paying the interest.

- <u>Reverse</u> Mortgages = have to be 62 yrs or older.

※ • Accelerated or Biweekly Payoff Program — if there is a fee.

Notes
monthly mortgage to bank
= $200k @ 5% = $10k tax

paid off = $10k @ 25% = $2500 tax
interest paid to bank

GUIDE
Dave Ramsey

BASIC WAYS TO FINANCE A HOME

- ___Conventional___ loans are usually through Fannie Mae and are privately insured against default.

- PMI is private mortgage insurance. = *Protects LENDER "forclosure insurance"*

- ___FHA___ (Federal Housing Administration) loans are insured by HUD—the federal government. = *low down payment but more expensive*

- VA loans are insured by the US Department of Veterans Affairs. = *can have a funding fee based on years service & length service in military*

- Owner financing is when you pay the owner over time, making him or her the mortgage holder. = *can be creative but get A CONTRACT (signed & notarized)*

" 100% OF FORECLOSURES HAPPEN ON HOMES *with a mortgage.* "

–DAVE RAMSEY

Notes Be: Cautious • Careful • Coherent
① Attack The DEBT !

CHALLENGES AND OPPORTUNITIES

* Non-traditional Credit →

If you do what we teach, your credit score will eventually hit zero, which means you'll need to find a mortgage lender that does MANUAL underwriting. via utility bills, rent, bank ~~account~~ account, etc.

When you owe more on your house than it is currently worth, you are upside down on your home. = Okay if nothing else changes

In a Short sale, the home is sold for less than the amount owed, and the lienholder agrees to accept the proceeds from the home sale as payment in full without recourse.

Willfully walking away from a mortgage—even though you have the money to make the payments—is called strategic default.

Notes

ANSWER KEY

Manual
Short

GUIDE
Dave Ramsey

SELLING A HOME

The most important aspect of preparation is attention to ___curb___ appeal.

The exposure through the ___Multiple___ Listing Service is worth it.

You should interview at least (three) real estate agents.

Have your agent do a detailed Comparative Market Analysis (CMA) to accurately price your home.

---

one-minute TAKEAWAY

- Paying off the townhome faster by ~~begin~~ getting rid of all debt can ~~be done~~ w/in 5 years, or be done w/in 5 years?

ANSWER KEY

Curb
Multiple

BUY A HOME *the Right Way*

Drew & Amy and Charles & Misty each put **20%** down on a **$200,000** home at a **4%** annual interest rate.

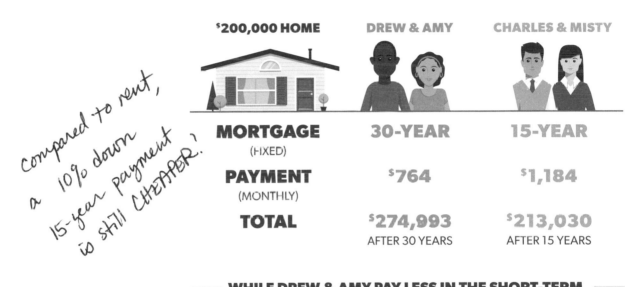

$200,000 HOME	DREW & AMY	CHARLES & MISTY
MORTGAGE (FIXED)	**30-YEAR**	**15-YEAR**
PAYMENT (MONTHLY)	$764	$1,184
TOTAL	$274,993 AFTER 30 YEARS	$213,030 AFTER 15 YEARS

Compared to rent, a 10% down 15-year payment is still CHEAPER!

WHILE DREW & AMY PAY LESS IN THE SHORT-TERM, THEY PAY HOW MUCH MORE OVERALL?

$_____

(Hint: $274,993 - $213,030)

Respond to the following questions:

1. Based on this example, would you rather be Drew and Amy or Charles and Misty? Why?

2. What could Charles and Misty do with the difference to build additional equity in their home? What would *you* do with the difference?

DISCUSSION

Whether you're in a group or online, be honest with your answers and remember to encourage one another!

 When you picture your dream home, what do you see? What parts of your home stand out and why are they important to you?

 Based on what you've learned from Dave and Chris, how do you know if you have too much house?

 Based on your answer to question two, do you need to make any adjustments to your housing situation? If so, what? Refinance? Sell? Buy? Throw more money at your mortgage?

 If you're a homeowner, think about life without a mortgage. What could you do with the extra money that's currently going toward payments? If you're renting, how do you feel about owning a home someday? How could you save up for one?

**KEEP THE
CONVERSATION
GOING!**

Answer these questions online in the Financial Peace community!

financialpeace.com

ACTION STEPS

It's time to live out what you just learned! Complete each of the action steps before the next lesson.

☐ **USE THE MORTGAGE CALCULATOR AND CONNECT WITH A REAL ESTATE ELP**
If you're a homeowner, use the Mortgage Calculator on **financialpeace.com** to figure out how much you're paying in interest over time—and to see how quickly you could pay off your home with extra payments. If you're ready to buy, use the calculator to see how much house you can afford, then connect with a real estate Endorsed Local Provider!

☐ **TAKE A LOOK AT YOUR BUDGET**
As part of your next budget, put some extra focus on your housing category. How much are you assigning to housing? Based on the lesson, do you have too much house?

☐ **INVESTIGATE A REFINANCE**
If you're in a bad mortgage like an Adjustable Rate Mortgage (ARM), you don't have to stay there—and you shouldn't! Research how you can refinance to a 15-year fixed mortgage.

☐ **COMPLETE YOUR FINANCIAL SNAPSHOT**
Now that you've completed eight lessons, use the Financial Snapshot tool at **financialpeace.com** to list your debt paid off, amount saved, and credit cards cut up or closed. If you're in a group, don't forget to transfer that information to your second Financial Snapshot card (page 120) and turn it in to your coordinator at the start of Lesson 9. Take a minute to celebrate your progress!

☐ **READ *PMI: NECESSARY OR NOT?* ON THE NEXT PAGE**
During the lesson, Chris described what PMI is all about. This article shares a little more about why it's not worth the trouble and how to knock it out once and for all.

PMI:
NECESSARY or Not?

We're going to save you $10,000 before this article ends. Ready?

You've worked the Baby Steps, done your research, and kept an eye on the housing market. You're ready to buy a home. If you can't put 100% down, you'll move through a mortgage approval process where you may encounter **Private Mortgage Insurance** (PMI).

Hold on a second. You might be asking yourself, *"Was this on the list of the seven insurances I need to have?"* We're glad you asked. The answer is no. And here's why.

AT A GLANCE

PMI = **PRIVATE MORTGAGE INSURANCE**

IF YOU PUT 20% DOWN, **YOU AVOID IT**

RATES RANGE FROM **.5–1.5% OF HOME LOAN AMOUNTS**

WHAT IS PMI?

PMI protects the lender. You're about to borrow a lot of money and your lender wants to make sure they get their money back if you can't make your payments and end up in foreclosure. Every year, there are between 500,000–1.5 million home foreclosures, so you can understand why lenders want insurance. Well, **PMI protects their investment.**

But here's the catch: You're the one who will be paying the insurance premiums—*not* them.

HOW MUCH DOES PMI COST?

PMI rates can range anywhere from .5–1.5% or more of your loan amount. For this example, let's use a 1% PMI and a $200,000 home loan amount.

At 1%, that would make your PMI $2,000 per year—an extra $166.67 per month added to your mortgage payment. After five years, PMI has added **$10,000** to the cost of your home. *There's that $10,000 you can save yourself.*

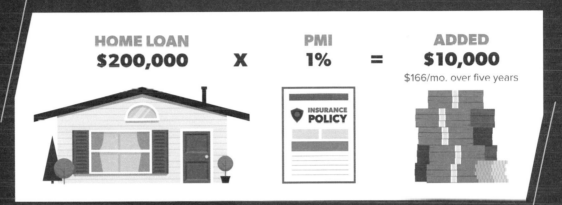

HOME LOAN
$200,000

X

PMI
1%

=

ADDED
$10,000
$166/mo. over five years

INSURANCE
POLICY

HOW CAN I AVOID PMI?

The easiest way to avoid PMI is to put at least **20% down** on your home. That completely eliminates PMI. If you *don't* put 20% down, PMI will be added to your loan automatically! You won't be able to get rid of it until you've paid down your loan enough to have 20–25% equity in your home. Basically, your loan-to-value amount has to be less than 80%.

HAVE A PLAN AND USE A PROFESSIONAL

If you're going to buy a home and get a mortgage, stick to this plan: Find a real estate agent you trust and get a 15-year fixed-rate mortgage with at least 10% down (though 20% is best), and make sure the total payments (including PMI) are no more than 25% of your take-home pay.

Let us help!

Ready to find a real estate agent you trust?
Go to **financialpeace.com** to find a real estate Endorsed Local Provider in your area who is ready to walk you through the home-buying process.

LESSON
09

" When you

LIVE

LIKE NO ONE ELSE,

later you can live

and give

LIKE NO ONE ELSE. "

—DAVE RAMSEY

THE
GREAT
MISUNDERSTANDING

KEY POINTS

God is a giver, and we best reflect His character when we give.

God gave us money to *manage*—not own. God owns it all.

When you live and give like no one else, you change yourself, your family tree, and your community.

GUIDE
Dave Ramsey

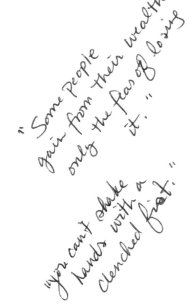

"Some people gain from their wealth only the fear of losing it."

"You can't shake hands with a clenched fist."

THE POWER OF GENEROSITY

You can do everything we teach and you will prosper, but if you don't understand this lesson, you will never have _financial_ _peace_.

The Great Misunderstanding—the paradox—is the mistaken belief that the way to have _more_ is to hold on _tightly_.

OWNERS AND MANAGERS

You and I are asset _managers_ for the Lord.

A _steward_ is a manager, not an _owner_.

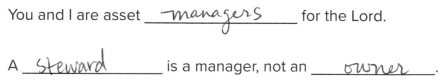

> **THE EARTH IS THE LORD'S, AND THE FULNESS** *thereof.*
>
> 📖 PSALM 24:1 (KJV)

Notes

WHAT HAPPENS WHEN WE GIVE?

Jesus talked more about ________________ than he did about love or grace in the New Testament.

Giving moves you to become less selfish________, and less selfish people have more of a tendency to prosper_________ in relationships and wealth.

Because we are designed in God's image, we are happiest and most fulfilled when serving and giving_________.

Notes

ANSWER KEY

Money
Selfish
Prosper
Giving

LESSON 9 //
THE GREAT MISUNDERSTANDING

WHY DO WE GIVE?

Giving is a reminder of ___ownership___.

Giving is praise and ___worship___.

Giving is ___spiritual___ warfare.

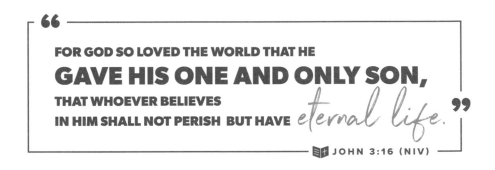

FOR GOD SO LOVED THE WORLD THAT HE
GAVE HIS ONE AND ONLY SON,
THAT WHOEVER BELIEVES
IN HIM SHALL NOT PERISH BUT HAVE *eternal life.*

📖 JOHN 3:16 (NIV)

Notes

//

TITHES AND OFFERINGS

The tithe is a tenth of your _____ *increase* _____ .

The Bible says to give your firstfruits, meaning off

the _____ .

The tithe is to go to your _____ church,

which provides the same function as the Old

Testament _____ .

_____ are different than the tithe. They are

above the tithe and are freely given from _____ .

Never give with the motive of having your

giving _____ .

one-minute TAKEAWAY

Give time as well as money!

Give a little until you can
GIVE A LOT

Giving changes you. We're not trying to be mushy or corny—it's a fact. You see, God is the ultimate giver. And when we give, we start to look more like Him.

1 Chronicles 29:14 (NIV) says, "Everything comes from you, and we have given you only what comes from your hand."

Everything we have comes from God. He owns it all! When He asks us to give, it's not because He needs our money. **His goal is not to reshape economics. His goal is to reshape our hearts.**

When you give your money, your time, and your talents to help and love other people, it doesn't change them—it changes you. And God's all about changing *you*.

That's what this whole journey has been about—changing you. Dave says, "As you change, your money changes. And as your money changes, you change."

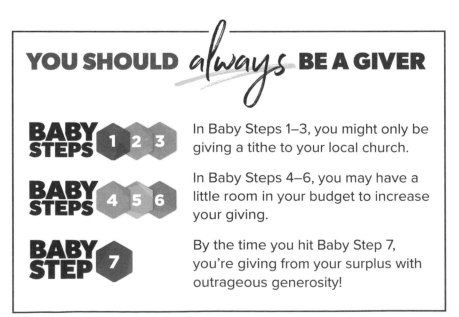

YOU SHOULD *always* **BE A GIVER**

BABY STEPS 1 2 3
In Baby Steps 1–3, you might only be giving a tithe to your local church.

BABY STEPS 4 5 6
In Baby Steps 4–6, you may have a little room in your budget to increase your giving.

BABY STEP 7
By the time you hit Baby Step 7, you're giving from your surplus with outrageous generosity!

WAYS YOU CAN START GIVING

In the space below, jot down some ideas about how you can start giving your money, time, and talents.

 ## MONEY

Budget a tithe (10% of your income) to your local church, off the top.

Give a 100% (or more!) tip at a restaurant.

• Give to a friend getting a new start — house — car — job — school

 ## TIME

Volunteer to be a Big Brother/Sister.

Sign up to serve at a local nonprofit or ministry you're passionate about.

 ## TALENTS

Lend your skills and volunteer to help build a home.

Put your mechanical talents to work and help fix your neighbor's car.

DISCUSSION

Whether you're in a group or online, be honest with your answers and remember to encourage one another!

 1 Remember, no matter where you are in the Baby Steps, giving should be the priority in your budget! How has this lesson helped you better understand the reason this is so important?

 2 Dave says that giving is the most fun you can have with money. How have you had fun with giving in the past? What made it so much fun?

 3 What keeps you from giving as much as you'd like to give? How does this lesson help you work through that hang-up?

 4 How does God's ownership of everything affect the way you think about what He's given you to manage?

KEEP THE CONVERSATION GOING!

Answer these questions online in the Financial Peace community!

financialpeace.com

ACTION STEPS

It's time to live out what you just learned! Complete each of the action steps before the next lesson.

☐ **GRATITUDE LEADS YOU TO CONTENTMENT**

Whether you're on Baby Step 2 or 7 and whether you have a little or a lot, God has given you something to manage. Rather than longing for bigger, better, and more, remember to practice **contentment**. Take time to celebrate how far you've come and to thank God for what He's given you. In the space below, write down three things you're thankful for!

1. _My family_
2. _My ~~so~~ friends_
3. _My job & my house._
   My health.

20% knowledge
80% effort & application

☐ **LOOK BACK AND CHARGE AHEAD**

If you've followed the plan, no matter where you are in the Baby Steps, your life should already look different than it did before you started *Financial Peace University*.

In the space below, list the top three things you've learned and then list your why—**the reason you refuse to quit**. This is why you decided to change, why you'll keep making sacrifices, why you won't give up when things get tough, and why you'll live like no one else so later you can live and give like no one else.

1. _Contentment is key._
2. _Persistence makes application successful._
3. _Take the ego out of it !!_

I will NOT give up because _I want the freedom that comes with ~~$~~ Financial Peace !!_

Your Story Began
WITH ONE DECISION...
TO CHANGE.

No matter where you started, you made it to where you are right now, and you *can* get to where you want to go next. And no matter how much longer it takes, you can get to Baby Step 7!

You've already taken the most difficult step—the first one.
The journey you're on didn't end on lesson nine. We're here to help you every step of the way. That's why your membership is so important!

YOUR MEMBERSHIP PERKS

Stay gazelle intense and work the plan with your Financial Peace membership. You have access to video lessons and new courses, tools, EveryDollar Plus, the member community, and financial coaches.

Attacking debt on Baby Step 2? Stay on track with the **Debt Snowball tool**.

Need a refresher on compound interest? Re-watch a lesson and find a **SmartVestor Pro** to start investing on Baby Step 4!

Need to talk through an obstacle you're facing? Connect with members in the **online community** or reach out to one of our **financial coaches.**

Interested in teaching your kids about money? Check out Dave and Rachel's video course, **Smart Money Smart Kids**.

Whatever you need to work the plan, you've got it! Plus, we're always adding new features to your membership.

Take advantage of your membership and keep going!

You got this.

LEARN MORE FROM
Dave, Chris, and Rachel!

We want to walk with you through every step of your financial journey. Stay connected daily with your **Financial Peace membership** and with our live events, books, podcasts, and shows.

Interested in hearing from us live? Reserve your seat for one of our upcoming live events at **daveramsey.com/events**. Or pick up one of the best-selling books from our team at **daveramsey.com/store/books**. No matter where you are in your journey, we have content, tools, and resources to help you along the way!

Hear from Dave every weekday on *The Dave Ramsey Show*—listen on the radio or on our app! (daveramsey.com/show)

Learn more from Chris on *The Chris Hogan Show* podcast. (chrishogan360.com)

Watch Rachel on *The Rachel Cruze Show*. (rachelcruze.com)

CHANGE LIVES AS A
FINANCIAL PEACE UNIVERSITY COORDINATOR

The two biggest reasons people become *Financial Peace University* coordinators is to stay motivated on their plan and to help others win with money! When you lead a *Financial Peace University* group, you get the opportunity to help others who are exactly where you started—people who are stressed, overwhelmed, and ready to make a change.

And you don't need to be out of debt or have any special training to lead a group. If you want to share *Financial Peace University* with others, then you're the perfect person to become a coordinator!

In fact, we make it easy to lead a group on your schedule.

YOU PICK THE TIME

Groups meet once a week for each lesson—at a time that works best for you.

YOU PICK THE DATE

Groups meet year-round. We'll help you set a date that's convenient for your schedule.

YOU PICK THE PLACE

Your group can meet at a church, local community center, or at your home.

Spread hope!

Visit **fpu.com/coordinator** to connect with someone from our team about starting and leading a group.

Spread hope to people right in your community and change lives as a *Financial Peace University* coordinator.

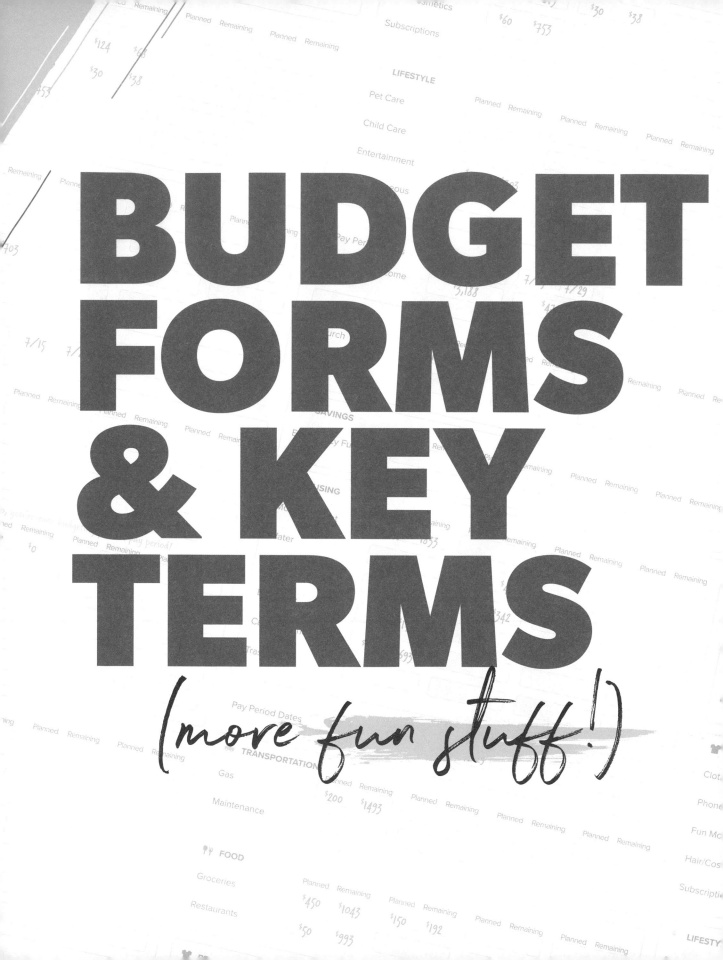

BUDGET FORMS & KEY TERMS

(more fun stuff!)

BUDGETING FORMS

Building new budgeting habits is a lot easier with the right tools. That's why we created **EveryDollar**—to easily make a plan for your money every month.

If you need a little extra guidance for budgeting weekly or budgeting for irregular income, the following two forms will help you out! Read through the step-by-step instructions on these example forms, then go to **financialpeace.com** to print out blank versions of these forms to fill out yourself.

Hey Nerds!

If you love pen-and-paper planning, you can find more forms— including extra budgeting forms—at **financialpeace.com**.

DIRECTIONS FOR
ALLOCATED SPENDING *Planning*

If you want to budget based on your pay period rather than the month, this form is for you! The four columns on this form represent the four weeks in a given month. If you're married, combine both of your incomes and then follow the steps below to allocate your spending.

1 **FILL OUT YOUR PAY PERIOD DATES AND PAY PERIOD INCOME.**

Your **pay period dates** are simply how long you'll go between paychecks. For example, if you get paid on the 1st and 15th, then your pay period for July would be 7/1 to 7/14. Your **pay period income** is how much you will be paid in that pay period. In our example, that will be $3,188.

Pay Period Dates	7/1 TO 7/14
Pay Period Income	$3,188

2 **FILL OUT YOUR PLANNED AND REMAINING COLUMNS.**

For this pay period, write down how much money **you plan to spend** in each category in the **Planned** column. In the **Remaining** column, keep a running total of how much of your income **you have left** for that pay period.

🏠 HOUSING	Planned	Remaining
Mortgage/Rent	$945	$2,243
Water	$25	$2,218

3 **PLAN FOR EACH CATEGORY ON THE LIST UNTIL YOU HIT ZERO.**

Plan for each category on the list until the Remaining column hits **zero**. When that happens, you're done budgeting for that pay period!

	Planned	Remaining
Saving	$100	$90
Giving	$90	$0

4 **IF YOU HAVE MONEY LEFT OVER...**

If you've planned for every category and you still have money left over in the Remaining column, **go back and adjust an area**, such as savings or giving, so that you spend every single dollar. **Every dollar needs a job to do!**

If the remaining column still has money, adjust an area!

		Planned	Remaining
Saving	+$50	$100	$200
Giving	+$60	$90	$110

ALLOCATED SPENDING FORM

Don't let this form scare you. Managing your money week to week happens here!

We've made an example form throughout the next couple of pages to help! **For a blank form, go to financialpeace.com.**

Pay Period Dates	7/1 TO 7/14	7/15 TO 7/29	TO	TO
Pay Period Income	$3,188	$472		

♥ GIVING

Income − Church = Remaining to budget this pay period

	Planned	Remaining	Planned	Remaining	Planned	Remaining	Planned	Remaining
Church	$410	$2,778						
Charity								

Remaining minus Planned, back & forth

🐷 SAVINGS

	Planned	Remaining	Planned	Remaining	Planned	Remaining	Planned	Remaining
Emergency Fund								

🏠 HOUSING

	Planned	Remaining	Planned	Remaining	Planned	Remaining	Planned	Remaining
Mortgage/Rent	$945	$1,833						
Water			$55	$417				
Natural Gas			$75	$342				
Electricity	$100	$1,733						
Cable/Internet	$40	$1,693						
Trash								

Pay Period Dates	7/1 TO 7/14		7/15 TO 7/29		TO		TO	

TRANSPORTATION

	Planned	Remaining	Planned	Remaining	Planned	Remaining	Planned	Remaining
Gas	$200	$1,493						
Maintenance								

FOOD

	Planned	Remaining	Planned	Remaining	Planned	Remaining	Planned	Remaining
Groceries	$450	$1,043	$150	$192				
Restaurants	$50	$993						

PERSONAL

	Planned	Remaining	Planned	Remaining	Planned	Remaining	Planned	Remaining
Clothing	$150	$843						
Phone			$124	$68				
Fun Money	$30	$813	$30	$38				
Hair/Cosmetics	$60	$753						
Subscriptions								

LIFESTYLE

	Planned	Remaining	Planned	Remaining	Planned	Remaining	Planned	Remaining
Pet Care								
Child Care								
Entertainment	$50	$703						
Miscellaneous								

Pay Period Dates	7/1 TO 7/14	7/15 TO 7/29	TO	TO

♥ HEALTH

	Planned	Remaining	Planned	Remaining	Planned	Remaining	Planned	Remaining
Gym								
Medicine/Vitamins								
Doctor Visits	$50	$653						

🏠 INSURANCE

When Remaining equals zero, you're done budgeting for this pay period!

	Planned	Remaining	Planned	Remaining	Planned	Remaining	Planned	Remaining
Health Insurance			$38	$0				
Life Insurance								
Auto Insurance	$88	$565						
Homeowner/Renter	$12	$553						
Identity Theft								

💳 DEBT

	Planned	Remaining	Planned	Remaining	Planned	Remaining	Planned	Remaining
Car Payment	$310	$243						
Credit Card 1	$150	$93						
Credit Card 2	$45	$48						
Credit Card 3								
Student Loan								
Medical Bill	$48	$0						
Personal Loan								

IRREGULAR INCOME *Planning*

If your income is different every month, use the Irregular Income Form along with your EveryDollar budget to make a plan for your money before the month begins. Follow the steps below to make a plan for any additional income you earn this month.

① FILL OUT YOUR BUDGET.

Fill out your budget based on **what you reasonably expect to bring home** for the month. If you aren't sure, use last year's lowest income month as your starting point.

● INCOME	
Paycheck	$3,500

② FILL OUT THE ITEMS COLUMN.

In the Items column, list out anything that didn't make it in your budget. These are **items you couldn't budget for,** but still need to be funded.

ITEMS

Main Card – Snowball

Hospital Bill – Snowball

Store Card – Snowball

③ LIST ITEMS IN PRIORITY ORDER.

Make sure your Items list is in the right order and keep a running total. Setting the right **priorities** is crucial here. For instance, a beach trip is not more important than paying off your debt!

PLANNED

$50

$460

$770

④ FILL IN ADDITIONAL INCOME.

When you get paid, write any **additional income** in the box. "Additional" means anything above and beyond what you planned on your budget.

ADDITIONAL IRREGULAR INCOME $1,500

⑤ SPEND UNTIL IT'S GONE.

Spend your money right down the list **until it's all gone.** You most likely won't make it all the way down the list. That's okay! That's why it's important to prioritize.

PLANNED	RUNNING TOTAL
$460	+ $510
$770	= $1,280
~~$500~~ $220	~~$1,280~~ $1,500

IRREGULAR INCOME FORM

This form helps you prioritize and plan for the items that didn't make it into your monthly budget. Follow the steps on the previous page to plan for your additional irregular income. We've made an example form below to help! **For a blank form, go to financialpeace.com.**

Any additional irregular income goes here.

ADDITIONAL IRREGULAR INCOME $1,500

List in priority order anything that didn't make it in your monthly budget.

Work back & forth, adding each budgeted item to the running total.

ITEMS	PLANNED	RUNNING TOTAL
Main Card - Snowball	$50	+ $50
Hospital Bill - Snowball	$460	= $510
Store Card - Snowball	$770	$1,280
Car Sinking Fund	~~$500~~ $220	~~$1,780~~ $1,500
Christmas Sinking Fund	$100	

KEY TERMS

Money shouldn't be complicated. **We make it simple.** We cover the words and phrases used in the last nine lessons in a way that's easy to understand.

SAVING & BUDGETING

Baby Steps: Dave Ramsey's proven seven-step path for winning with money

Budget: A monthly plan, either on paper or digital, that puts every dollar you make into a specific category

Compound Interest: Interest that gets paid on both the money you put in (your principal) and on the interest you've already earned

Four Walls: The most basic expenses you need to cover to keep your family going: your food, your utilities, your shelter, and your transportation

Interest Rate: An extra percentage you pay to a lender for money you borrow

Money Market Mutual Fund: Basically, a savings account you can open with a mutual fund company instead of a bank; it usually earns a little more interest than a bank savings account thanks to short-term mutual fund investments.

Sinking Fund: Setting aside money over time so you can buy something with cash—for example, saving $400 a month for 10 months to buy a $4,000 car

Zero-Based Budget: A monthly budget that puts every dollar you earn into specific categories—so when your income is subtracted from your expenses, you come up with zero.

DEBT

Annual Percentage Rate (APR): The amount that borrowed money costs you each year; the APR includes your interest rate and other related fees you have to pay on a loan

Debt Snowball: List of all debts (except your house) from smallest to largest. Make minimum payments on all of them while you attack the smallest debt by paying as much on it as you can. Once it's paid off, "roll" the money you were paying on it to your payment on the next smallest debt. Keep this going until you've paid off the last, largest debt.

FICO Score: Number used to evaluate your "credit worthiness;" it's really an "I love debt" score that's based on your debt history, how much debt you currently have, how long you've been in debt, new debt, and the kind of debt you have.

Introductory Rate: A marketing tool that offers a lower-than-normal interest rate during the early stages of a loan; it's a rate designed to attract new customers, and it almost always goes up over time.

Navient: A student loan service that split off from Sallie Mae in 2013

Sallie Mae: Originally a government program known as the Student Loan Marketing Association (SLMA), it's still the largest private student loan lender in the country.

SPENDING

Brand Recognition: A marketing term that measures just how aware customers are of particular brands

Buyer's Remorse: Feeling of doubt or regret about a purchase soon after making it

Caveat Emptor: Latin term that means "let the buyer beware"

Financing: Using debt to buy something; can also refer to the attractive terms and conditions companies use to market what they want you to buy with debt

Impulse Purchase: Buying something without thinking about the bigger picture

INSURANCE

Cash Value Life Insurance: Basically, a permanent life insurance policy (as opposed to a term policy) that charges high premiums and puts money in a savings account with low return rates; also referred to as whole life, universal life, and variable life. Never buy this kind of life insurance.

Claim: The paperwork you send to an insurance company when you want them to cover a loss

Coverage: The amount of protection you get from an insurance company when you suffer a loss

Deductible: The money you pay out of pocket before insurance benefits kick in

Health Savings Account (HSA): A tax-free savings account that sets aside money for medical expenses

Liability: The amount of your financial obligation when you're found at fault in an accident

Policy: In insurance, a contract that explains what is covered and what is not

Premium: The regular payment you make to an insurance company to ensure coverage; can be a monthly, quarterly, or annual payment

Stop Loss: For insurance, the maximum amount of out-of-pocket expense you pay each year

Term Life Insurance: Life insurance that remains in force for a certain period (a term); if someone depends on your income, you need term life insurance

INVESTING

401(k): A retirement savings plan through a business where employees set aside tax-deferred income from each paycheck

401(k) Match: A company benefit where an employer "matches" a percentage of what an employee sets aside for retirement

403(b): A tax-favored retirement plan for public school and non-profit employees

Roth 401(k): An employer-sponsored retirement plan funded with after-tax money; since taxes have already been paid, the account grows tax-free

Roth IRA: A personal retirement account that grows tax-free because it's funded with after-tax dollars

Direct Transfer: Moving the money from one tax-deferred retirement plan into another approved plan; because none of the money goes to you, there are no immediate tax liabilities or penalties. Also known as a "rollover." Often used when moving from one company to another

Diversification: Spreading money among different kinds of investments to minimize risk

Individual Retirement Arrangement (IRA): A tax-deferred plan where workers can save some of their income for retirement; as the plan's value grows, the money isn't taxed until it's taken out.

Liquidity: A measure of how easy it is to get to your money from an account; the easier the access, the more liquid it is

Mutual Fund: An investing tool where a group of people combine their money to create a fund of several different stocks

Risk: The level of uncertainty about the potential returns on an investment

Rollover: See "Direct Transfer"

Share: How much an individual investor owns in a publicly traded company

MORTGAGE

Adjustable-Rate Mortgage (ARM): A mortgage interest rate changes—usually going up—periodically; allows banks to transfer risk to consumers through higher interest rates

Curb Appeal: How nice a house looks to someone passing by

Comparative Market Analysis (CMA): The estimated value of property based on what similar properties in the area have sold for

Equity: How much of property you own compared to how much you still owe on it; usually seen in terms of how much of a mortgage amount you've actually paid

Fannie Mae (FNMA): The Federal National Mortgage Association, a privately owned company that deals in mortgages

Fixed Rate: An interest rate that never changes over time; considered a much better option than an adjustable rate

Inflation Hedge: An asset that increases in value over time and counters a rising inflation rate

Multiple Listing Service (MLS): A computer program used by real estate agents to search updated property listings

Mortgage: A loan arrangement made for buying real estate; the property serves as collateral for the loan

Private Mortgage Insurance (PMI): Insurance that protects a lender from a borrower who defaults on a mortgage; usually required when the borrower has paid less than 20% of the mortgage value

Principal: For investments, the original amount of money put in the investment; for loans, the actual payoff amount of a loan, not including interest or other fees

GIVING

Firstfruits: The first produce gathered during a harvest, typically given as an offering to God in the Bible

Great Misunderstanding: The mistaken belief that you get more by holding tightly to what you have instead of keeping an open hand

Offering: A gift given above and beyond the tithe; freewill gifts given without a sense of obligation or expectation

Stewardship: The act of managing the resources God has given each of us for His glory

Tithe: A gift of 10% of one's income, given to the local church

$27,275.97 in 7 mnths 5 days!
Andrea and Joshua Hahn
We did this for you Maverick!
Thanks, Dave!

We're DEBT FREE !!
191,300.00 in 10 months
We SOLD our Rental ☺
Thank-you Lord !!
Jesse ♡ Carol

We are debt free!
$123,495
Ron & Colleen Barger
THANK YOU DAVE !!!

Nate, Laura, Nathan,
Luke, and Rachel
McDonell
$96,000 in 37
months!!!
"We're Debt Free!"

$249k in 4 yrs!
Andrew, Kelly, AJ Weisner
Columbus, Indiana

Jarrod & Stefanie Staggs
122k in 36 months!!
DEBT FREE!!! WOOOO!

FREEDOM!!!
Living like no
one else so
later we can
live like no
one else!
22K/18 mos
cash flowing
20k for school!
Sebastian &
Mackenzie
Sanchez

Ben & Alyson Baxter
$80,000 in 36 months

Andy From Inwood, WV
$206,000 in 44 months
Love the Financial Peace